The Scarecrow Author Bibliographies Series

Bibliographies of the following authors are forthcoming:

E. M. Forster
Howard Nemerov
William Faulkner
Benjamin Disraeli

Robert Greene Criticism: A Comprehensive Bibliography

by

Tetsumaro Hayashi
**Assistant Professor of English
Ball State University**

With an Introduction by Louis Marder,
Editor of The *Shakespeare Newsletter*

The Scarecrow Press, Inc.
Metuchen, N.J.   1971

The Scarecrow Author Bibliographies Series, No. 6

Dedicated to
Akiko and Richard H. Hayashi,
Mrs. Rokuno Sakuratani,
and
Drs. Didier and Lotte Graeffe

Other Books by the Same Author

Arthur Miller Criticism (1969)

John Steinbeck: A Concise Bibliography (1930-1965) (1967)

A Looking Glasse for London and England, an Elizabethan Text (1970)

Sketches of American Culture (1960)

Monograph by the Same Author

A Textual Study of a Looking Glasse for London and England by Thomas Lodge and Robert Greene (1970)

Journal Edited by the Same Author

Steinbeck Quarterly (1968-)

Table of Contents

Introduction

The true art of enumerative bibliography is founded
on a passionate interest in one's subject plus a commensurate
determination to assist others in their investigation in the
same area. Indirectly, a bibliography may stimulate a
broader interest in the subject when it falls into the hands
of someone who thumbs through its pages and discovers by
serendipity a subject that arouses his curiosity, or a weak-
ness in an area where he is, or may become, competent to
shed new light.

The problem in preparing a bibliography is related
to the aims of the compiler coupled to the aims of his publisher who must eventually assume the cost of publication.
No bibliographer worth his salt will intentionally omit an
important reference, although he may be compelled by
necessity to omit some that may be considered minor. The
main problem here is to decide between what is major and
what is minor. Who is to say that a one-page citation is
less important or pertinent than a long reference? Who has
not sometimes been more inspired and stimulated by a single
paragraph in a tangential book on the subject, than a full
chapter in a relevant volume? Dare a carping critic scan
the pages of a bibliography and note derisively that there
are many references to single pages, thinking that the compiler has merely sought to give thickness rather than usefulness to the compilation? Will he wonder whether the
work in hand is an allusion book rather than a bibliography?

Dr. Samuel A. Tannenbaum told me twenty-three years ago that for his inclusiveness he was damned by some who did not want to be bothered by references to peripheral and non-scholarly material. It was his task, he thought, to assemble the citations. With them, the user could do as he pleased.

It is always easier to find fault than to be constructive. Dr. Johnson remarked long ago that a critic is one who may grow great at small expense. Bibliographers cannot be similarly damned. They do not seek greatness, but rather to be useful. Some bibliographers have become great by dealing with the old and unusual, making their work sought after by rare book dealers as well as scholars. Other bibliographers with ample time and scholarly acumen have annotated every reference to provide a vade mecum of scholarship. Others, and they include the majority, have been content to function as explorers and as guides to simplify the travels of those who would like to spend more time reading and studying than ransacking libraries and their card catalogs to compile what is available.

One of the greatest problems is that of inclusion and exclusion. For ordinary purposes a short research bibliography of major books and articles may be sufficient. For more extensive scholarship a comprehensive bibliography is required. For broad and profound scholarship, an exhaustive bibliography is absolutely essential in order to preclude the danger of missing, possibly, the one link in the chain of argument or rebuttal and proof or negation.

Exhaustiveness is the ideal, but impractical to achieve because of time and money. This ideal will be achieved only when the libraries of the world have been exhaustively classified and coded for computer storage and retrieval. The bibliographer of today can only sigh when he thinks that a hundred years hence the research that took years of his life to assemble will be accomplishable in a few minutes, and that the computer-supplied references will always be current, up to the date of the search.

In the English library world, so far as I am aware, only the Library of Congress and the British Museum attempt exhaustive collections. But even they cannot compete with the exhaustiveness of specialized collections like The Folger Shakespeare Library, and even these cannot hope to encompass everything. Some libraries may even exercise their prerogative to evaluate a book and not include it if it is deemed of no value.

With bibliographies it is the same, and the same dangers ensue. When a scholar-student finds an unlisted item, he may think he has made a new discovery. How is he to know that the volume <u>was</u> known, but not included? What thorough scholar will desist from seeking or reading the unlisted work in order to make his own judgment? Personally I have never seen a bibliography which included <u>excluded</u> books, but I have heard of some where the compilers' value judgments resulted in listing the contents as books of great value, some value, or no value.

All of these problems have probably occurred to and have been met by Dr. Tetsumaro Hayashi. His bibliography was not an idly conceived work, but a labor of love which grew out of studies for his own dissertation. The mere reference to the number of citations will tell the user that it is the longest bibliography of Robert Greene in existence. The scholar will be able to test for himself the inclusiveness of the contents.

I have been instrumental in helping my former

student and now valued friend to several dozen references. The compiler expects that Robert Greene specialists may be able to supply more.

Several valuable features enhance the usefulness of this work. The chronology of the life and works provides perspective. The inclusion of the primary Greene materials and their location (originally the compilation of Professor Johnstone Parr and his colleagues), and the thorough classification of the remaining contents beyond the scope of his predecessor, Dr. Tannenbaum, are welcome features. Seemingly repetitious, but better than the usual "see also" references, is the duplication of citations under all the classifications to which they appertain. The inclusion of the sources of the bibliography (III B) will enable the user to seek for additional citations there in the years subsequent to the publication of the compilation.

For me, the bibliography, to have been ideally perfect, would have had to provide capsule summaries of the contents, citations to book reviews where relevant, comments from the reviews which might guide me in evaluation, and a small comprehensive list of the important foreign work on the subject. But, so far as I know, no such work exists for any author, and to have produced such an impossible dream would have entailed more years than Dr. Hayashi has to spare. It was thoughtful of him to think that his long bibliographical labors on Greene should not be repeated by other scholars so he offers his compilation to the public. It is better to be thankful for what he has accomplished than to find fault for the little he may have omitted. Now he has new worlds to conquer.

Louis Marder, Editor,
The Shakespeare Newsletter
University of Illinois at
Chicago Circle
Chicago, Illinois

Preface

In 1939 Samuel A. Tannenbaum pointed out: "It is a sad commentary on human unreasonableness that though Robert Greene is entitled to a prominent place in the history of English literature and the English language by virtue of his genius, he is most frequently the subject of discussion only because of his ill-natured and jealous attack on Shakespeare." He also contended that many students of English literature were not aware of the fact that Greene was "one of the most original, most versatile, and most prolific writers of the period, one who did much to make the age of Elizabeth the most illustrious era in England's annals."[1] One would judge from the contemporary scholarly output, however, that the situation had considerably improved by 1969.

Professor Johnstone Parr, a distinguished Robert Greene scholar now at Kent State University, in cooperation with his associates then of the Shakespeare Institute at the University of Birmingham, England, published both List of Editions, Copies, and Locations of the Works of Robert Greene[2] in 1958 and Instructions to Editors of the Works of Robert Greene[3] in 1959. Although Dr. Parr's ambitious project of editing the texts of Robert Greene's works has not yet been completed, his enthusiasm and leadership seem to have begun to stimulate Robert Greene studies in recent years.

This renewed interest necessitates a more up-to-date and more comprehensive bibliography to supplement Dr.

Tannenbaum's Robert Greene: A Concise Bibliography (1939),
which happens to be, as far as I know, the sole "booklet-
length" (58 pages) bibliography published to date in this
field. Furthermore, Irving Ribner's Tudor and Stuart
Drama, a selective bibliography, (New York: Appleton-
Century-Crofts, 1966), devotes only two pages to Robert
Greene. The latest bibliography entitled The University
Wits: Lyly, Greene, Peele, Nashe and Lodge by Robert C.
Johnson (London: Nether Press, 1969) is arranged
chronologically from 1935 to 1965 and contains only 135
items on Greene. When I worked on my Ph.D. dissertation on Thomas Lodge and Robert Greene under the direction
of Professor Johnstone Parr, I had to employ, in addition
to Tannenbaum's bibliography, many reference guides such
as the PMLA Annual Bibliography, Abstracts of English
Studies, the International Index to Periodicals, Studies in
Philology Annual Bibliography, and Dissertation Abstracts.
To save the scholars' time, energy, and frustration I
decided to compile Robert Greene Criticism, a comprehensive bibliography.

In my book I drastically revised the organization of
Dr. Tannenbaum's bibliography in order to be more
functional, and included more selected critical materials
published after 1939. I do not claim this to be an exhaustive bibliography, however. If I have failed to include
any significant and worthy articles, pamphlets, monographs,
Ph.D. dissertations, and others, I would welcome and
appreciate pertinent information. I firmly believe that a
bibliography of this kind, like any other comprehensive
scholarly endeavor, needs cooperation and assistance from
all scholars working in the field.

Many of the sources presented here were discovered

personally. For many others I have used standard
bibliographical aids as well as the selected bibliographical
guides prepared by various scholars of Elizabethan drama.
I owe them a great deal, but I am especially indebted to
two bibliographies: Dr. Tannenbaum's and Dr. Parr's. I
greatly depended upon them and they inspired me to compile
this comprehensive bibliography.

I attempted to include exclusively English language
materials in this book. Generally speaking, I followed both
Kate T. Turabian's bibliographical method and that of the
MLA Style Sheet. However, I took the liberty of adding,
revising, omitting, or simplifying some of the entries
whenever I found it necessary or beneficial for the users
of this compilation.

I wish to take this opportunity to thank a number of
people who have generously helped me with this project. The
librarians of the Ball State University, the Indiana University, the Kent State University, the Huntington Library in
San Marino, California, and the Folger Shakespeare Library
in Washington, D.C. have rendered their professional
service to me. Dr. Louis Marder of the University of
Illinois at Chicago Circle was kind enough to proofread
the manuscript, and he gave me many invaluable suggestions.
I would like to stress the fact, however, that although he
has read the manuscript, I alone am responsible for any
imperfections in this book. Both Dr. Dick A. Renner,
present Chairman, and Dr. Thomas H. Wetmore, former
Chairman of the English Department, Ball State University,
allowed me to duplicate some of the rare materials through
the departmental Xerox copying service. Dr. Louis
Marder, distinguished editor of the Shakespeare Newsletter

at the University of Illinois (Chicago Circle), called my attention to a number of extremely important Greene materials and meticulously directed this project by making both his widespread knowledge and his outstanding personal library available to me. Furthermore, he generously endorsed and graced my book by writing an Introduction.

Dr. Ralph Shaw, President of the Scarecrow Press, Inc., who believed in the value of this comprehensive bibliography, accepted this manuscript for publication, and his associate, Mr. Eric Moon, Executive Officer of the Press, competently edited my manuscript. Dr. Johnstone Parr, who had directed my Ph.D. dissertation from which this book is derived as a by-product, kindly allowed me to include his entire list of all the extant original quartos of Robert Greene's works, which were originally published in Parr's and others' bibliographical pamphlet, A List of Editions, Copies and Locations of the Works of Robert Greene (Shakespeare Institute, Birmingham, England, 1958). My wife, Akiko Hayashi, has never failed to give me the most needed moral support while I was compiling this bibliography. Both Miss Catherine Daughhetee and Mrs. Nancy Chalfant, my secretaries, efficiently typed and retyped the manuscript for me. To these scholars, bibliographers, research librarians, editors, and friends I owe special thanks for their assistance, advice, wisdom, and encouragement.

Tetsumaro Hayashi
Ball State University
Muncie, Indiana
January 1, 1970

Notes

1. Tannenbaum, Samuel A. Robert Greene: A Concise Bibliography. (New York: Privately printed, 1939), p. ii.

2. Parr, Johnstone, and others. List of Editions, Copies and Locations of the Works of Robert Greene. (Birmingham, England: Shakespeare Institute, University of Birmingham, 1959).

3. Parr, Johnstone, and Shapiro, I. A. Instructions to Editors of the Works of Robert Greene. (Shakespeare Institute, 1959).

Chronology of Robert Greene (1558-1592)

1558 (July 11) Robert Greene born at Norwich and
     baptized.

1575 Entered St. John's College, Cambridge as a sizar.

1578 Received B.A., St. John's College.

1580 (October 3) Mamillia (Pt. I) (S.R.).

1580 (October 3) A Mirrour or Looking-Glasse for the
     Ladies of England (S.R.).

1583 Received M.A. from Cambridge.

1583 (September 6) Mamillia (Pt. II) (S.R.).

1584 The Carde of Fancie.

1584 Morando (Pt. I) (No entry).

1584 (April 11) Gwydonius (S.R.).

1584 (August 13) Arbasto (S.R.).

1585 A Funeral Sermon (No entry).

1585 Planetomachia (No entry). Called himself a "student
     of phisicke." Returned to Norwich to marry (?).

c.1585 (the end of 1585 or early in 1586) Married to "a
     gentleman's daughter of good account"
     (Repentance) and seemed to have settled for
     awhile at Norwich.

1586 Deserted his wife and child, and went to London(?).
     Began first association with the players.

1586 (August 8) Morando, the Tritameron of Love (S.R.).

1587	Alphonsus, King of Arragon.
1587	Morando, (Pts. I and II) published.
1587	(June 11) Farewell to Folly (S.R.).
1587	(June 26) Penelope's Web (S.R.).
1587	(September 18) Euphues His Censure to Philautus (S.R.).
1588	Pandosto: The Triumph of Time (or Dorastus and Fawnia) (No entry).
1588	(March 29) Perimedes the Black-Smith (S.R.).
1588	(July) Received Oxford M.A.
1588	(December 9) Alcida (S.R.).
1589	Ciceronis Amor (No entry).
1589	Friar Bacon and Friar Bungay.
1589	(February 1) Spanish Masquerado (S.R.).
1589	(August 23) Menaphon (Greenes Arcadia).
1589	(September 22) Scillaes Metamorphosis (S.R.).
1590	Francescos Fortunes (No entry).
1590	George-a-Greene.
1590	Greenes Never Too Late.
1590	Greenes Vision (No entry).
1590	(January 9) Orpharion (S.R.).
1590	(March 8, 27, April 19, and June 7) A Looking-Glasse for London and England with Thomas Lodge was performed according to Henslowe's Diary.
1590	(April 15) The Royal Exchange (S.R.).
1590	(November 2) Greenes Mourning Garment (S.R.).

1591   Conny-Catching (Pts. I and II).

1591   Greenes Farewell to Folly.

1591   James IV.

1591   Orlando Furioso.

1591   (December 6) A Maidens Dreame* (Poem) (S.R.).
             (*His only extant poem which is not part of a
             work of fiction).

1591   (December 13) Conny-Catching (Pt. III) (S.R.).

1591   (December 13) A Notable Discovery of Cosenage
             (S.R.).

1592   A Disputation Between a Hee Conny-Catcher and a
             Shee Conny-Catcher (No entry).

1592   Henslowe's note of a performance of Friar Bacon as
             a rival to Marlowe's Doctor Faustus.

1592   (February 7) Conny-Catching (Pt. III) (S.R.).

1592   (February 17) Dedication of Lodge's Euphues
             Shadow (S.R.).

1592   (February 21) Orlando Furioso performed in
             Henslowe's theater by the Admiral's and Lord
             Strange's men.

1592   (April 21) The Defence of Conny-Catching (S.R.).

1592   (July 1) Philomela (S.R.).

1592   (July 21) A Quip for an Upstart Courtier (S.R.).

1592   (August 21) The Blacke Bookes Messenger (S.R.).

1592   (September 2 or 3) Died poverty-stricken in
             London. Buried on September 4 in the New
             Churchyard, near Bethlehem Hospital.

1592   (September 20) Greene's Groatsworth of Wit, in
             which appears an attack on Shakespeare (S.R.).

1592	(October 6) The Repentance of Robert Greene, Master of Arts (S.R.) (Posthumous.)
1592	(December 4) Gabriel Harvey's Fovre Letters and Certaine Sonnets: especially touching Robert Greene and other parties by him abused.
1593	Greenes Funeralls.
1593	Greenes Newes both from Heaven and Hell.
1593	Mamillia (Part II).
1593	(December 7) Orlando Furioso (S.R.).
1594	The Anatomie of Love's Flatteries.
1594	The Historie of Orlando Furioso.
1594	The Honorable Historie of Friar Bacon and Friar Bungay.
1594	Selimus.
1594	(March 5) A Looking Glasse for London and England with Thomas Lodge (S.R.).
1594	(May 14) The Scottish Historie of James IV (S.R.).
1594	James IV, the earliest known copy.
1599	Alphonsus King of Aragon.
1599	The Comicall Historie of Alphonsus, King of Aragon.
1599	George-a-Greene, The Pinner of Wakefield.
1602	Greenes Ghost Haunting Connie-Catchers.
1606	A Pair of Turtle Doves.
1608	Greenes Carde of Fancie.
1610	Greenes Arcadia, or Menaphon.
1617	Alcida.

PART I: PRIMARY MATERIAL

A. Original Quartos (Earliest Extant Editions)

Alcida

STC	Date	
12216	1617	Bodleian (Malone 573)
		Bodleian (Rawl. 379)
		BM
		Folger
		Folger (Jolley)
		Harmsworth
		Harvard (Freeling-Paine-White)
		HEH
		Morgan (Griswold-Irwin)

Alphonsus

STC	Date	
12233	1599	Folger (Clawson)
		HEH (Bridgewater)
		V&A (Dyce)

Arbasto

STC	Date	
12217	1584	BM (Isham, made-up, imp.)
		HEH (Davis, made-up)
12218	1584	(Same as 12217)
12219	1589	HEH (White)
12220	1594	HEH (Christ Church-Lyte-Corser-Britwell)

STC	Date	
12221	1617	Bodleian (Malone 574)
		HEH (Utterson-Halliwell)
12222	1626	BM (Wright-George III)

The Black Bookes Messenger

STC	Date	
12223	1592	Bodleian (Malone)
		HEH (Heber-Freeling-
		Britwell)

Ciceronis Amor

STC	Date	
12224	1589	Folger (Nassau-Heber-
		Corser-Huth-White)
		HEH (Heber-Britwell)
12225	1597	BM
12226	1601	Chapin Library
		Harvard (Corser-White;
		lacks D3)
		HEH (Bridgewater)
		Rosenbach (8/30 Britwell)
12227	1605	BM
		Cambridge University
		Library
12228	1609	BM
		Harvard (McKee-White)
		Newberry Library, Chicago
12229	1611	BM (imp.)
		Folger
12230	1616	Birmingham University
		Bodleian (Malone)
		BM
		HEH (Hoe)
		Sion College
		V&A (Dyce)
12231	1628	BM
		Folger
		Harvard (White)
12232	1639	Bodleian
		Morgan

Dedication of Thomas Lodge's Euphues Shadow

STC	Date	
16656	1592	BM Folger (White?) HEH Trinity College, Cambridge Yale

The Defence of Conny-Catching

STC		
5655		BM(imp.; A2-3 belong to STC 12280).
5656		HEH (Huth)

The Second Part of Conny-Catching

STC	Date	
12281	1591	HEH (Halliwell-Corser- Huth)
12282	1592	Bodleian (Malone) Pforzheimer (Steevens- Roxburghe-Heber- Freeling-Britwell- Clawson)

The Third and Last Part of Conny-Catching

STC	Date	
12283	1592	Bodleian (Malone) HEH (Heber-Freeling- Britwell)
12284		(See 11094; end of present list)

A Disputation

STC	Date	
12234	1592	Bodleian (Malone) HEH (Heber-Freeling- Britwell)

STC	Date	
12235	1615	Bodleian
12236	1615	Bodleian (Douce)
		Bodleian (Malone)
		BM
12237	1621	Bodleian (Wood)
		Guildall Library
12238	1637	Bodleian (Tanner)
		BM
		Folger
		Harmsworth (Britwell)
		HEH (Huth)
		Pepysian Library (WAJ's C6 a mistake for L6?)
		Sion College

Euphues His Censure to Philautus

STC	Date	
12239	1587	BM
		HEH (Gardner-Corser-Huth)
		Advocates Library, Edinburgh
12240	1634	Bodleian (Malone)
		BM
		Eton
		Harvard (White; lacks A1)
		HEH (Hoe)
		Morgan (Griswold)
		Trinity College, Cambridge
		Yale

Farewell to Folly

STC	Date	
12241	1591	BM (Gilchrist-Heber?)
		Folger
		HEH (Phelps-Heber-Britwell)
12242	1617	Bodleian (Douce; imp.)
		Bodleian (Malone 572)
		BM
		Cambridge University Library

Chapin (Heber-Huth-Jones)
Folger (Corser-Freeling-
   White?)
Folger (Ives-Lefferts)
Harmsworth (Britwell)
Harvard
HEH (Hoe)
V&A (Dyce)
Vienna

A Funeral Oration

STC	Date	
12354	1585	HEH

Greenes Ghost Haunting Connie-Catchers

STC	Date	
12243	1602	BM (Freeling-Corser)
		Cambridge University Library (imp.)
		Folger (Ives-Lefferts)
		Morgan
		Pforzheimer (Huth-Clawson)
12244	1626	Bodleian (Malone)
		BM
		Folger
		Folger (Pearson)
		Harvard (Clawson-Hager)
		HEH (Jolley-Brindley-Halliwell*) (*Hoe)
		Trinity College, Cambridge
		White (in Folger?)
		Yale

George-a-Greene

STC	Date	
12212	1599	Bodleian (Malone)
		BM (Garrick)
		C.W. Clark (Daniel-Huth-HEH-Jones)

STC	Date	
		Folger (Rhodes-Devonshire- HEH-Young-Lefferts) HEH (Bridgewater) Pforzheimer (Mostyn 13y- Clawson) V&A (Dyce) Wise (=Ashley=Mostyn 450) Worcester College, Oxford
12213		Bodleian Folger (Harmsworth?) Harmsworth HEH (Hoe)

Greenes Newes Both From Heaven and Hell

STC	Date	
12259	1593	BM Cock Library, Durham (WAJ crosses out; Library dispersed in 1920's and location of books now unknown) Folger Harmsworth (Huth) HEH (Christ Church-Lyte- Corser-Britwell) PRO, Dublin Wise

Groatsworth of Wit

STC	Date	
12245	1592	BM Folger (Fenn-Frere-White)
12246	1596	Folger (imp.) HEH (Jolley-Corser-Huth) Pforzheimer (Wrangham- Britwell)
12247	1617	Bodleian (Wood) BM Chapin Library (Halliwell- Huth) Folger Folger (Locker Lampson)

STC	Date	
		Ham House
		University of Illinois
		Rosenbach (Corser-White)
		Vienna)
12248	1621	Bodleian
		BM
		Folger
		Folger (Warwick)
		Harmsworth
		HEH (G. D. Smith)
		Trinity College, Cambridge
		V&A (Dyce)
12249	1629	Bodleian (Malone)
		Boston Public Library
		HEH (Gardner-Britwell)
12250	1637	Bodleian
		BM
		Folger (Kershaw?)
		Morgan (Utterson-Irwin)
		Sion College
		Trinity College, Cambridge
		Worcester College, Oxford
		Yale

Gwydonius, The Card of Fancie

STC	Date	
12262	1584	HEH (Freeling-Britwell)
12262.1	1587	Folger (Heber-Pyne)
12263	1593	Bodleian (Malone 573)
12264	1608	Bodleian (Mason)
		BM
		Folger (White second copy, lacks H2-3, Kl-4)
		Harvard
		HEH (Huth)
		V&A (Dyce)
		Yale (Constable-Cunliffe)

James the Fourth

STC	Date	
12308	1598	BM Folger (Huth) HEH (Bridgewater) V&A (Dyce)

A Looking Glasse

STC	Date	
16679	1594	HEH (Kemble-Devonshire)
16680	1598	Bodleian (2 copies) BM University of Chicago (but cf. Greg, no. 188d) HEH
16681	1602	BM (Smith-Hever-Fitchett-Marsh-Locker-Lampson)
16682	1617	Bodleian Boston Public Library (T. P. Barton, 1873) BM (2 copies) Folger (Mitford-White or Clawson?) HEH Harvard Library of Congress Pepysian Library, Cambridge Pforzheimer Library V&A (Dyce) Yale (Mitford-White or Clawson?)

A Maidens Dream

STC	Date	
12271	1591	Folger Lambeth Palace

Menaphon

STC	Date	
12272	1589	BM (imp., lacks A3) Folger (Brindley-Heber- Britwell-White) HEH (Hoe)
12273	1599	Bodleian Sion College
12273.1	(1605)	Trinity College, Cambridge (imp., lacking A)
12274	1610	BM Folger (Cunliffe) Harvard (Locker Lampson- White) HEH (Huth-Jones)

12275	1616	Bodleian (Crynes)
		Bodleian (Malone)
		BM
		Folger (Corser-Britwell)
		Harvard
		HEH (Hoe)
		Pforzheimer (Freeling-
		   Corser-McKee-Jones-
		   Clawson)
		Vienna State Libraries
		Yale (White, according to
		   WAJ)
		(Pforzheimer Cat. says
		   two other copies in
		   hands of booksellers,
		   including Huth copy; a
		   copy was to be sold at
		   Sotheby's, 16 Dec. 1958,
		   lot 277)

Morando (I)

STC	Date	

12276	1584	Bodleian (Tanner 217)
		BM (imp., A only; B
		   onwards is STC 12277)
		Pforzheimer (Heber-
		   Freeling-Britwell-
		   Jones-Clawson)

STC   Date

                              HEH (Osterley Park--Lock-
                                  er Lampson-Hoe)

                    Morando (I and II)

STC   Date

12277   1587   Bodleian (Douce; wanting
                                  first ten and last two
                                  leaves)
                              Bodleian (Malone 572)
                              BM (George III)
                              BM (see STC 12276 above)
                              HEH (Lyet-Corser-Huth-
                                  White)

                    Mourning Garment

STC   Date

12251   1590   Cambridge University
                                  Library (imp.)
12252   1616   Advocates Library,
                                  Edinburgh
                              Bodleian (Malone)
                              Bodleian (Wood)
                              BM
                              Folger (Huth; lacks C4)
                              Harvard (Caldicott-
                                  Britwell)
                              HEH (Jolley-H.V.Jones)
                              Morgan
                              A.S.W. Rosenbach (imp.,
                                  A1, K4, blank)
                              [This library is now
                                  dispersed since
                                  Rosenbach's death].
12252   1616   Vienna
                              White (Corser?)

                    The Myrrour of Modestie

STC   Date

12278   1584   BM (C.53.a. 37)
                              HEH (Jolley-Britwell)

<u>Never Too Late--Francescos Fortunes</u>

STC	Date	
12253	1590	BM (Both parts, both imp.)
		HEH (Christ Church-Lyte-
		George Smith-Britwell)
		(Part I only)
12253. 1	1600	Folger (Dalrymple)
12254	1600	Bodleian (Malone)
		Sion College
12254. 1	1602	Folger
12255	1607	BM (North-Heber)
		HEH (White)
12255. 1	1611	V&A (Dyce)
12256	1616	Bodleian (Douce; imp.)
		BM (Tite; imp.)
		BM (Wright-George III;
		imp)
		Folger
		Harvard (Jolley-Locker-
		Lampson-White; imp.)
		HEH
		Pforzheimer (Alexander
		Young-Henkels
		Miscellany-Clawson)
		Sion College (imp.)
		Dulwich College
		Norwich Public Library
		Rosenbach (Forman; imp. ,
		8/ 30) (-Folger ?)
		Trinity College,
		Cambridge (doubtful)
		University of Kansas
		Warrington Public Library
12256. 1	1602?	BM (identical with 12257. 1)
		Folger (or 12257. 1)
		HEH (Britwell)
12257	1621	Bodleian (Douce)
		Folger (Brindley-Thorpe)
		Harvard (Jolley Locker
		Lampson-White)
		Lambeth Palace
		Pforzheimer (Clawson)
		Trinity College, Cambridge
		(date shaved off...WAJ:
		I suspect this incorrect.
		J. Parr)

STC	Date	
12257.1	1630?	BM
		Harvard (Sewell-White)
12258	1631	Folger (Freeling-Huth)
		HEH (Corser-Huth-Chew-Hazlitt-Britwell)
		Newberry Library, Chicago
		Trinity College, Cambridge
		University of Texas

A Notable Discovery of Cosenage

STC	Date	
12279	1591	Bodleian (Wood; imp.)
		BM
		HEH (Britwell)
12280	1592	Bodleian (Malone)
		Folger (Westminster)
		Gonville and Caius College, Cambridge
		HEH (Steevens-Roxburghe-Heber-Freeline-Corser-Huth; A2-3 lacking, in their place A2-3 of STC 5656.)
		V&A (Dyce)

Orlando Furioso

STC	Date	
12265	1594	BM
		Folger (Heber-Perkins-Britwell-White)
		HEH (Bridgewater)
		V&A (Dyce; imp.)

Orpharion

STC	Date	
12260	1599	Bodleian (Malone)
		BM (Wright-George III)
		Harvard (White)
		HEH (Christ Church-Lyte-Corser-Huth)

STC   Date

> Morgan (Frederickson-
> Griswold-Irwin)
> Pforzheimer (Freeling-
> Britwell-Clawson)
> Vienna National Library
> Pforz. Cat. lists one other,
> unlocated copy)

A Paire of Turtle Doves

STC	Date	
11094	1606	Bodleian (Douce) HEH (Bowle Steevens- Brand-White Knights- Heber Corser-Huth) Pforzheimer (Sykes-Free- ling-Britwell-Clawson)

Pandosto

STC	Date	
12285	1588	BM (Wright, imp.)
12286	1592	Folger (White)
12287	1595	HEH (Newdigate, imp.)
12288	1607	Bodleian (Malone)
12288.1	1609	Folger
12289	1614	BM
12289.1	1619	HEH (Mistake for 12289?)
12289.2	1621	Vienna National Library
12290	1629	Bodleian
12291	1632	BM
12292	1636	BM Folger HEH
12292.1	Folger	Folger (Date shaved off) Warwick Castle?

Penelopes Web

STC	Date	
12293	(1587)	Bodleian (Malone) HEH (Heber-Britwell)

STC	Date
12294	1601	BM Harvard (White) HEH (Freeling-Huth) V&A (Dyce)

Perimedes the Blacksmith

STC	Date
12295	1588	Bodleian (Malone) BM HEH (Steevens-Roxburghe- Heber-Freeling- Britwell)

Philomela

STC	Date
12296	1592	Corpus Christi College, Oxford Harvard (Bright-Britwell- Jones-White) HEH (North-Heber- Britwell; imp.)
12297	1615	Bodleian (Malone) BM Folger Harvard (Freeling-Corser- McKee-White) HEH (Walpole-Freeling- Britwell) Vienna
12298	1631	BM (Wright-George III) Cambridge University Library (Sanders) Folger (Jolley--Utterson- Gardner-Huth-Quaritch) HEH (Hoe) Pforzheimer (Mildmoy- Clawson)

Planetomachia

STC	Date	
12299	1585	Bodleian (Malone 573)
		Bodleian (Tanner 253 (2))
		BM (Halliwell)
		BM (Steevens-Heber- Freeling-Utterson; C. 39. e. 67)
		HEH (Bolland-Britwell)

A Quip

STC	Date	
12300	1592	HEH (Henry White-Heber- Britwell)
12300a	1592	Bodleian
12301	1592	Westminster Abbey Library
12301a	1592	BM (95. b. 19)
		BM (Wise-Ashley; P. 5785, Ash. 833)
		Folger (Locker Lampson)
		Harvard (W. A. White)
		HEH (Bridgewater)
		Norwich Public Library
		A. S. W. Rosenbach
12302	1606	HEH (Corser-Huth)
12303	1620	Bodleian (Douce)
		Bodleian (Malone)
		BM
		Cambridge University Library
		University of Chicago Library
		Folger
		Harmsworth
		Harvard (Griswold-Brit- well-Lefferts-White)
		HEH
		Morgan
		V&A (Dyce)
12304	1622	Bodleian
		Chapin Library (Huth; date shaved off)

STC	Date	
		HEH
		"G. 7" (? ?See WAJ)
12305	1635	Boston Public Library
		(Brindley)
		BM
		Folger
		Harmsworth (Britwell)
		Harvard (Paine-White)
		HEH (Gainsford?)
		Quaritch 436
		St. John's College,
		Cambridge (Bagford?)
		Sion College
		Trinity College,
		Cambridge (imp.)

The Repentance

STC	Date	
12306	1592	Bodleian (Malone)

The Royal Exchange

STC	Date	
12307	1590	Bodleian (Wood)
		BM
		Chetham Library,
		Manchester
		Folger
		HEH (Herbert-Roxburghe-
		Heber-Freeling-
		Britwell)

Selimus

STC	Date	
12310a	1594	Advocates Library,
		Edinburgh, (Bute)
		Bodleian (Malone)
		Boston Public Library
		BM
		Folger (Clawson)

STC	Date	
		Harvard (Mitford-White)
		HEH (Bridgewater)
		University of Illinois
		V&A
		V&A (Dyce)
		Yale
12310b	1638	Advocates Library, Edinburgh
		Bodleian (Malone)
		BM
		HEH (Bridgewater)

The Spanish Masquerado

STC	Date	
12309	1589	Advocates Library, Edinburgh
		Bodleian (Malone)
		BM (Christ Church-Lyte-Huth-Wise)
		BM (Wright-George III)
		Chapin Library
		Chatsworth
		Folger (Clawson)
		Harvard (Corser-Freeling-White)
		Trinity College, Cambridge (imp.)
		V&A (Dyce)
		Yale
12310	1589	BM (Grenville)
		BM (Old Royal)
		Harvard (White)
		HEH (Hoe)
		Morgan (Griswold)
		Pforzheimer (Utterson-Britwell)
		Texas University (Wrenn?)

Notes

This list was rearranged and quoted from Johnstone
Parr and others' List of Editions, Copies, and Locations of
the Works of Robert Greene (Birmingham, England:
Shakespeare Institute, University of Birmingham, 1958) with
Professor Parr's permission.

Most of these original quartos are now available in
microfilms. Be sure to check English Books 1475-1640:
Consolidated Cross Index By STC Number (Ann Arbor:
University Microfilms, 1956) and use the STC numbers.

The statement in parenthesis after the library indi-
cates who originally owned the quarto. It is meaningful
only when a certain library owns two identical quartos, but
both came from different sources.

Bodleian (Dyce) = a quarto that now belongs to
Bodleian Library, but originally it was owned by Dyce.

Key to Abbreviations Used in This List

Advocates = Advocates Library, Edinburgh, Scotland

Birmingham = Birmingham University Library, Birmingham,
    England

BM = British Museum Library, Great Russell St.,
    Bloomsbury, London, England

Bodleian = Bodleian Library, University of Oxford, Oxford,
    England

Boston = Boston Public Library, Boston, Massachusetts

Cambridge = Cambridge University Library, Cambridge,
    England

Chapin = Chapin Library, Williamstown, Mass. (STC has
    this incorrectly as Virginia)

Chatsworth = the famous mansion in Derbyshire of the
    dukes of Devonshire. Contained a fabulous library of
    books and manuscripts

Chetham = Chetham Library, Hunt's Bank, Manchester 3, England

Chicago = University of Chicago Libraries, 1116 E. 59th St. , Chicago, Illinois

Clark = C. W. Clark, a private library

Cook = Cook Library, Durham, England

Corpus Christi = Corpus Christi College Library, University of Oxford, Oxford, England

Dulwich = Dulwich College Library, London, England

Eton = Eton College Library, Eton, England

Folger = Folger Shakespeare Library, Washington, D. C.

Gonville & Caius = Gonville and Caius College Library, University of Cambridge, Cambridge, England

Guildhall = Guildhall Library, Library of the Corporation of London, England

Ham House = a Museum and Art Gallery in London

Harmsworh = Sir R. L. Harmsworth, a private collection in England

Harvard = The Houghton Library, Harvard University, Cambridge, Massachusetts

H. E. H. = Henry E. Huntington Library and Art Gallery, San Marino, California

Illinois = University of Illinois Libraries, Urbana, Illinois

Kansas = University of Kansas Libraries, Lawrence, Kansas

Lambeth = Lambeth Palace Library, Lambeth, England

Library of Congress = Washington, D. C.

Morgan = The Pierpont Morgan Library, 33 East 36th St. , New York, N. Y.

Newberry = Newberry Library, 60 West Walton Street,
    Chicago, Illinois

Norwich = Norwich Public Libraries, Bethel Street,
    Norwich, England

Pepysian = Pepysian Library, Magdalene College,
    Cambridge, England

Pforzheimer = Carl H. Pforzheimer Catalogue

PRO = Public Record Office, Dublin, Ireland

Quaritch = a famous second-hand bookseller in London,
    Bearnard Quaritch, 1819-1899. At one time he produced
    A General Catalogue of Old Books and Manuscripts (1887-
    89; Index 1892). "436" is an item number in his
    catalogue. (J. Parr)

Rosenbach = A. S. W. Rosenbach, a private library (Now
    dispersed since his death, according to Dr. Louis
    Marder, Editor of the Shakespeare Newsletter)

St. John's = St. John's College Library, Cambridge,
    England

Sion = Sion College Library, Victoria Embankment, London,
    England

STC = A Short-Title Catalogue of Books Printed in England,
    Scotland and Ireland of English Books Printed Abroad
    1475-1640) compiled by A. W. Pollard and G. R. Red-
    grave. London: Bibliographical Society, 1926.

Texas = University of Texas Libraries, Austin, Texas

Trinity = Trinity College Library, Cambridge, England

V & A = Library of the Victoria and Albert Museum, South
    Kensington, S. W. 7, England

Vienna = Vienna National Library, Vienna, Austria

WAJ = William A. Jackson's Notes for Revised STC (photo-
    stats at the Shakespeare Institute and University of

Alabama, from Professor Jackson.... Professor Parr's note)

Warrington = Warrington Public Library, Warrington, Lancashire, England

Warwick Castle = Warwick Castle Library, Warwick, England

Westminster = Westminster Abbey Library, S. W. 1, England

White = W. A. White Catalogue (1926)

Wise = Thomas James Wise (1859-1937), bibliographer, collector, editor, who formed the great Ashley Library in England. This seems to have been acquired by the British Museum in 1937. There is a Catalogue of the Library (1922-30), 11 volumes..... Professor Parr's note.

Worcester = Worcester College Library, Oxford, England

Yale = Yale University Libraries, New Haven, Connecticut

B.   Collected Works and Modern Editions

1.   Baskerville, C. R. et al (eds.). Friar Bacon in Elizabethan and Stuart Plays. New York: Holt and Co. , 1934. pp. 247-284.

2.   ---- et al (eds.). George-a-Greene in Elizabethan and Stuart Plays. pp. 285-306.

3.   Bell, Robert (ed.). The Annotated Edition of the English Poets. London: J. W. Parker, 1845.

4.   ---- . The Poems of Robert Greene, Christopher Marlowe, and Ben Jonson. London: G. Bell, 1889.

5.   Bratchell, D. F. (ed.). "An Edition of the Planetomachia and Penelope's Web of Robert Greene," Unpublished Ph. D. dissertation, University of Birmingham, 1955-56. [Index, Vi, 9].

6.   Cellini, Benvennto (ed.). Robert Greene: Friar Bacon
      and Friar Bungay, John of Bordeaux in The Second
      Part of Friar Bacon. LaNuova Italia, Firenze
      (1952) [Reviewed in YWES, 34 (1953), 154].

7.   Clugston, George Alan. "A Looking Glasse for London
      and England, By Thomas Lodge and Robert Greene.
      A Critical Edition, " Unpublished Ph. D. dissertation,
      University of Michigan, 1967.

8.   Collins, John Churton (ed.). The Plays and Poems of
      Robert Greene.   2 volumes. Oxford: Clarendon
      Press, 1905.

9.   Dickinson, Thomas H. (ed.). The Complete Plays of
      Robert Greene.   London: T. F. Unwin, 1909.
      (Mermaid series).

10.   ----. Robert Greene.   London: T. F. Unwin; New York:
      Scribner's, 1909.

11.   Dodsley, R. (ed.). Friar Bacon and Friar Bungay in
      Select Collection of Old English Plays (London),
      VIII (1825-27), 163-240.

12.   Dyce, Alexander (ed.). Collected Plays and Poems of
      Robert Greene.   2 volumes.   London: (n. p.), 1831.

13.   ----. The Dramatic and Poetic Works of Robert Greene
      and George Peele.   London: W. Pickering, 1883.

14.   Farmer, John S. (ed.). A Looking Glasse for London
      and England.   Amersham, 1914.   (Tudor Facsimile
      Texts).

15.   Gosse, Edmund W. (ed.). A Looking Glasse for
      London and England in The Complete Works of
      Thomas Lodge (1580-1623).   Volume IV.   New
      York: Russell and Russell, 1963 (Reprint of the
      Hunterian Club edition).

16.   Greg, W. W. (ed.). A Looking-Glasse for London and
      England By Thomas Lodge and Robert Greene 1954.
      London: Malone Society, 1932.

17.   Grosart, Alexander B. (ed.). The Life and Complete
      Works in Prose and Verse of Robert Greene.   15

volumes. London: Huth Library, 1881-86; New
York: Russell and Russell, 1964.

18.   Harrison, G. B. (ed.). Elizabethan and Jacobean
Quartos: Robert Greene, M. A., A Notable Dis-
covery of Coosnage 1591, The Second Part of
Conny-Catching 1592. New York: Barnes and
Noble, 1966 (c. 1922).

19.   ----. (ed.). Robert Greene, M. A., Groats-Worth
of Witte, The Repentance of Robert Greene, 1592.
New York: Barnes and Noble, 1960 (c. 1922).

20.   ----. (ed.). Robert Greene, M. A., The Blacke
Bookes Messenger 1592; Cuthbert Conny-Cather;
The Defence of Conny-Catching 1592. New York:
Barnes and Noble, 1966 (c. 1922).

21.   ---- (ed.). Robert Greene, M. A., The Third and
Last Part of Conny-Catching, and A Disputation
Between a Hee Coony-Catcher and a Shee Conny-
Catcher. New York: Barnes and Noble, 1966
(c. 1922).

22.   Hayashi, Tetsumaro. A Looking Glasse for London
and England by Thomas Lodge and Robert Greene,
An Elizabethan Text. Metuchen, N. J. : Scarecrow
Press, 1970.

23.   Hebel, J. William, et al (eds.). Tudor Poetry and
Prose. New York: Appleton-Century-Crofts,
1953.
Contents:

Greene's Prose, pp. 939-956:

A Notable Discovery of Cozenage (abridgment)

The Third Part of Conny-Catching (selection)

Groats-worth of Wit (selection).

24.   Heywood, Jasper (ed.). Greenes Groatsworth of
Witte. London: Bell, 1617, (Q).

25.   Hibbard, G. R. (ed.). Three Elizabethan Pamphlets.
London: Harrap, 1951. [YWES, 32(1951), 159].

Contents: Robert Greene, <u>The Third and Last</u>
<u>Part of Conny-Catching</u>; Thomas Nashe, <u>Pierce</u>
<u>Penilesse his Supplication to the Devil</u>; Thomas
Dekker, <u>The Wonderful Year</u>.

26.   Horsman, E. A. (ed.). <u>The Pinner of Wakefield.</u>
Liverpool: University Press, 1956 (English Reprint Series).

27.   Judges, A. V. (ed.). <u>The Elizabethan Underworld.</u>
New York: E. P. Dutton, 1930.

28.   Jusserand, J. J. <u>The English Novel in the Time of</u>
<u>Shakespeare.</u> tr. from the French by Elizabeth
Lee. 1895.

29.   Keltie, John Scott (ed.). <u>Friar Bacon and Friar</u>
<u>Bungay</u> in <u>The Works of the British Dramatists.</u>
Edinburgh: W. P. Nimmo, 1870. pp. 76-96.

30.   Lee, Elizabeth. See Jusserand, J. J.

31.   Lodge, Thomas. <u>A Looking-Glasse for London and</u>
<u>England</u>, 1594. with Robert Greene. See W. W.
Greg.

32.   MacIlwraith, Archibald K. (ed). "<u>Friar Bacon</u>" in
<u>Five Elizabethan Comedies.</u> New York: Oxford
University Press, 1934.

33.   McMillan, Mary Evelyn. "An Edition of <u>Greenes</u>
<u>Vision</u> and <u>A Maidens Dreame</u> by Robert Greene,"
Unpublished Ph. D. dissertation, University of
Alabama, 1960.

34.   Pickering, W. <u>The Dramatic Works of Robert Greene.</u>
2 volumes. London: (n. p.), 1831.

35.   Rowland, Samuel (ed.). <u>Greenes Ghost.</u> London:
for R. Jackson and I. North, 1602. (Q)

36.   Seltzer, Daniel (ed.). <u>Robert Greene: Friar Bacon</u>
<u>and Friar Bungay.</u> Lincoln: University of Ne-
braska Press, 1963 [<u>YWES,</u> 44(1963), 167].

37.   Winny, James (ed.). <u>Pandosto</u> in <u>The Descent of</u>
<u>Euphues, Three Elizabethan Romance Stories.</u>

Cambridge: University Press, 1957.

C.   Poems In Anthologies

38.   Bullen, A. H. (ed.). Lyrics from the Dramatists of
        the Elizabethan Age. London: Privately printed,
        1901.

        Contents: From A Looking Glasse for London and
        England: "Do Me Right and Do Me Reason";

        From Perimedes the Black-Smith: "Wanton Youth
        Reproved," and "Phillis and Coridon," pp. 233-235;

        From Menaphon: "In Love's Dispraise," p. 237;
        "Weep Not, My Wanton," p. 238; "The Eagle and
        the Fly," p. 239; "Doron's Description of Samela,"
        p. 240;

        From Ciceronis Amor: "Jealousy," p. 241; "Venus
        Victrix," p. 242 "Love Schooled," p. 243;

        From The Orpharion: "Love's Treasury," p. 244;

        From the Mourning Garment: "The Shepherd's
        Wife's Song," p. 245;

        From Never Too Late: "N' oserez Vous, Mon Bel
        Ami?" p. 247;

        From Francesco's Fortunes: "Eurymachus' Fancy
        in the Prime of His Affection," p. 249; "Radagon
        in Dianam," p. 254; "Mullidor's Madrigal," p.
        255.

        From The Farewell to Folly: "A Mid Content,"
        p. 256;

        From Philomela: "Philomela's Ode," p. 257;
        "Philomela's Second Ode," p. 258; "Sonnet," p.
        261; "Answer," p. 261;

        From the Groatsworth of Wit: "Lamilia's Song,"
        p. 262; "Miserrimus," p. 263.

39.   Hebel, J. William, et al (eds.). Tudor Poetry and
       Prose. New York: Appleton-Century-Crofts,
       1953.

       Contents: From Menaphon: "Doron's Description
       of Samela," pp. 150-151; "Doron's Jig," p. 151;
       "Sephestia's Song to Her Child," pp. 151-152.

       From Greene's Never Too Late: "The Palmer's
       Ode," p. 154;

       From Greene's Farewell to Folly: "Sweet Are
       the Thoughts," pp. 154-155;

       From Greene's Orpharion: "Cupid abroad was
       lated," pp. 155-156.

40.   Lucie-Smith, Edward (ed.). The Penguin Book of
       Elizabethan Verse. Baltimore: Penguin, 1965.

       Contents: "Shephestia's Song," p. 132; "Infida's
       Song," pp. 133-135; "Sonnet or Ditty," pp. 135-
       136.

41.   Rollins, Hyder E. and Baker, Herschel (eds.). The
       Renaissance in England. Boston: D.C. Heath,
       1954.

       Contents: From Arbasto: "In Time We See That
       Silver Drops," p. 380;

       From Morando: "The Fickle Seat Whereon Proud
       Fortune Sits," p. 380;

       From Perimedes: "Obscure and Dark is All the
       Gloomy Air," p. 380; "In Cypress Sat Fair Venus
       By a Fount," p. 380; "Fair Is My Love for April
       in Her Face," p. 381;

       From Ciceronis Amor: "When Gods Had Framed
       the Sweet of Women's Face," p. 381;

       From Greene's Farewell to Folly: "Sweet Are
       the Thoughts That Savor of Content," p. 381;

       From Philomela: "Philomela's Ode That She Sung
       in Her Arbor," p. 381.

42.   Taylor, Warren and Hall, Donald (eds.). <u>Poetry in</u>
          <u>English</u> New York: Macmillan, 1963. "Sephastia's
          Song to Her Child," p. 93.

PART II: SECONDARY MATERIAL

A.   Criticism By Individual Work And Related Subjects

(1) Alphonsus (Play, 1599)

43.   Chambers, E. K.   The Elizabethan Stage.   4 volumes.
       Oxford: Clarendon Press, 1961 [c. 1923].   IV, 2.

44.   Collins, J. Churton (ed.). , The Plays and Poems
       of Robert Greene.   Oxford Clarendon Press, 1905.
       I, 70-76.

45.   Gayley, Charles Mills.   Representative English
       Comedies.   New York: Macmillan, 1930.   I, 403-
       405.

46.   Jordan, John Clark.   Robert Greene.   New York:
       Octagon Books, 1965 [c. 1915]. pp. 174-177, 190-
       193.

47.   Muir, Kenneth.   "Robert Greene as Dramatist," in
       Essays on Shakespeare and Elizabethan Drama in
       Honor of Hardin Craig.   ed. Richard Hosley.
       Columbia: University of Missouri Press, 1962.
       pp. 46-47.

48.   Ribner, Irving.   "Greene's Attack on Marlowe: Some
       Light on Alphonsus and Selimus," SP 52, (1955),
       162-176 [YWES, 36(1955), 129].

49.   Van Dam, B. A. P.   "Greene's Alphonsus," English
       Studies, 13 (1931), 129-142.

(2) The Carde of Fancie   (Romance, 1608)

50.   Dent, Robert W.   "Greene's Gwydonius: The Carde
       of Fancie: A Study in Elizabethan Plagiarism,"
       HLQ, 24 (1961), 151-162 [YWES, 42 (1961), 155].

51. Hornat, Jaroslav. "Two Euphuistic Stories of Robert
     Greene: The Carde of Fancie and Pandosto,"
     Philologica Pragensia, 6 (1963), 21-35.

52. Jones, F. L. "Another Source for the Trial of Chi-
     valry, Robert Greene's The Carde of Fancie,"
     PMLA, 47 (September 1932), 688-690.

53. Jordan, John Clark. Robert Greene. New York:
     Octagon Books, 1965 [c. 1915]. pp. 65-66.

(3) Conny-Catching (Repentance Pamphlet, 1592)

54. Baker, Ernest A. "The Conny-Catching Pamphlets,"
     in The History of the English Novel. London:
     Witherby, 1934-39, II, 135-152.

55. Brown, G. A. "Robert Greene's Pamphlets of Conny-
     Catching," Academy, 77 (August 8, 1914), 87.

56. Chandler, F. W. "Conny-Catching Pamphlets," The
     Literature Roguery. Boston: Houghton, Mifflin,
     1907. I, 93-105.

57. Day, Martin S. History of English Literature to
     1660. Garden City, N. Y.: Doubleday, 1963. p.
     232.

58. Hibbard, G. R. (ed.). Three Elizabethan Pamphlets.
     London: (* on the Third and Last Part of Conny-
     Catching; Reviewed in TLS, February 29, 1952.
     p. 162).

59. Johnson, Francis R. "The Editions of Robert
     Greene's Three Parts of Conny-Catching: a Biblio-
     graphical Analysis," Library, 9 (1954), 17-24.

60. Jordan, John Clark. Robert Greene. New York:
     Octagon Books, 1965 [c. 1915]. pp. 105-106,
     passim.

61. Miller, Edwin Haviland. "A Bestseller Brought up
     to Date: Later Printings of Robert Greene's A
     Disputation Between a He Conny-Catcher and a She
     Conny-Catcher (1592)," PBSA, 52 (1958), 126-
     131.

62.   ----. "Further Notes on the Authorship of The De-
        fense of Conny-Catching (1592)," N & Q, 197
        (1952), 446-451.

63.   Pearson, Terry P. "The Defence of Conny-Catching,"
        N & Q, 204 (April 1959), 151-153.
        (* On a passage which may refer to Phillip
        Stubbes.)

64.   Shapiro, I. A. "An Unsuspected Early Edition of The
        Defence of Conny-Catching," Library, 18 (June
        1963), 88-112.

        (4). Farewell to Follie (Romance, 1591)

65.   Jordan, John Clark. Robert Greene. New York:
        Octagon Books, 1965 [c. 1915]. Passim.

66.   Sanders, Norman. "Greene's 'Tomliuoling'," N & Q,
        207 (June 1962), 229-230.

67.   ----. "Robert Greene's Way with a Source," N & Q,
        14 (March 1967), 89-91.

        (5) Friar Bacon and Friar Bungay
            (Play, 1594)

68.   Bayley, A. R. "Robert Greene and Roger Bacon,"
        N & Q, 108 (November 7, 1903), 361-362.

69.   Bradbrook, M. C. The Growth and Structure of
        Elizabethan Comedy. Baltimore: Penguin Books,
        1963. p. 80.

70.   Brooke, C. F. Tucker. The Tudor Drama. Hamden,
        Conn. : Archon Books, 1964 [c. 1911], pp. 266-
        268.

71.   Cellini, Benvenuto. Friar Bacon and Friar Bungay:
        John of Bordeau or the Second Part of Friar Bacon.
        Firenze: La Nuova Italia, 1952. (* Reviewed by
        G. Baldini in Convivium, 23 (1955), 473-476.)

72.   Chambers, E. K. The Elizabethan State. 4 vols.
        Oxford: Clarendon Press, 1961 [c. 1923] II, 114;
        III, 328; IV, 12.

73.   ----. "Note on Friar Bacon," RES, I (April 1925),
          186.

74.   Collins, J. Churton (ed.).   The Plays and Poems
          of Robert Greene.   II, 1013.

75.   Day, Martin S.   History of English Literature to
          1660.   Garden City, N. Y.: Doubleday, 1963.
          Passim.

76.   Ellis-Fermor, Una.   "Marlowe and Greene: A Note
          on Their Relationship as Dramatic Artists," in
          Studies in Honor of T. W. Baldwin.   Urbana:
          University of Illinois Press, 1958.   pp. 136-149.

77.   Empson, William.   "The Function of the Double
          Plot," Shakespeare's Contemporaries, ed. Max
          Bluestone and Norman Rabkin.   Englewood Cliffs,
          N. J.: Prentice-Hall, 1961.   pp. 34-35 [Originally
          in his Some Versions of Pastoral.   London:
          Chatto & Windus, 1935.   pp. 27-34].

78.   Fleay, Frederick G.   "On the Date of Friar Bacon,"
          Dr. Faustus and Friar Bacon, ed.   A. W. Ward.
          Oxford: (n. p.), 1901.   pp. clxii-clxxiii.

79.   Gayley, Charles Mills.   Representative English Com-
          edies.   New York: Macmillan, 1930.   I, 411-415.

80.   Holzknecht, Karl J.   Outlines of Tudor and Stuart
          Plays.   New York: Barnes and Noble, 1963.   pp.
          100-117.   (On Friar Bacon, George-a-Greene, and
          James IV.)

81.   Jordan, John Clark.   Robert Greene.   pp. 180-181,
          195-196.

82.   McCallum, J. D.   "Greene's Friar Bacon and Friar
          Bungay," M. L. N., 35 (April 1920), 212-217.

83.   MacLaine, A. H.   "Greene's Borrowings from His
          Own Prose Fiction in Bacon and Bungay and
          James IV," PQ, 30 (January 1951), 22-29.

84.   McNeir, Waldon F.   "Traditional Elements in the
          Character of Greene's Friar Bacon," SP, 45
          (April 1948), 172-179.

85.   Mills, J. W.   "Friar Bacon," Academy, 32 (February
      12, 1887), 116.

86.   Muir, Kenneth.   "Robert Greene as Dramatist," in
      Essays on Shakespeare and Elizabethan Drama in
      Honor of Hardin Craig, ed. Richard Hosley.
      Columbia: University of Missouri Press, 1962.
      pp. 48-50.

87.   Parrott, Thomas M. and Ball, Robert H.   A Short
      View of Elizabethan Drama.   New York: Scribner's
      1958. [c. 1943]. pp. 71-72.

88.   Reed, Robert R. , Jr.   The Occult in the Tudor and
      Stuart Stage.   Boston: Christopher Publishing
      House, 1965. pp. 101-106.

89.   Round, Percy Z.   "Greene's Materials for Friar
      Bacon and Friar Bungay," MLN 21 (January 1926),
      19-23.

90.   Schelling, F. E.   "Doctor Faustus and Friar Bacon,"
      Nation, 101 (July 1, 1915), 12-13.

91.   Seltzer, Daniel (ed.).   Robert Greene, Friar Bacon
      and Friar Bungay.   Lincoln: University of Ne-
      braska Press, 1963.   pp. ix-xxi.

92.   Thomas, W. J.   (ed.).   "The Famous Historie of
      Fryer Bacon," Early English Prose Romances
      London: Nattaliand Bond, 1907. pp. 285-328.

93.   Towne, Frank.   "White Magic in Friar Bacon and
      Friar Bungay," MLN, 67 (January 1952), 9-13.

94.   Ward, A. W.   Marlowe's Faustus and Greene's Friar
      Bacon.   Oxford: Clarendon Press, 1901. (4th
      edition: Old English Drama).

95.   West, Robert H.   "White Magic In Friar Bacon,"
      MLN, 67 (1952), 449-450. (*Comments on the
      article by Frank Towne's "White Magic in Friar
      Bacon. " MLN, 67 (1952), 9-13.)

96.   ----.   "Reply to 'White Magic in Friar Bacon and
      Friar Bungay'" by F. Towne. " MLN, 67 (Nov.
      1952), 499-500.

(6) <u>George-a-Greene</u> (Play, 1599)

97.   Bald, R. C.   "<u>The Locrine and George-a-Greene</u>:
        Title Page Inscriptions," <u>Library</u> (London), 15
        (December 1934), 295-305.

98.   Bradbrook, M. C.   <u>The Growth and Structure of
        Elizabethan Comedy</u>.   Baltimore: Penguin Books,
        1963.   pp. 80-81.

99.   Chambers, E. K.   <u>The Elizabethan Stage</u>.   4 volumes.
        Oxford: Clarendon Press, 1961 [c. 1923].   IV,
        14.

100.   Collins, J. Churton (ed.).   <u>The Plays and Poems of
        Robert Greene.</u>   Oxford: Clarendon Press, 1905.
        II, 159-179.

101.   Gayley, Charles Mills.   <u>Representative English
        Comedies.</u>   New York: Macmillan, 1930.   I,
        418-420.

102.   Holzknecht, Karl J.   <u>Outlines of Tudor and Stuart
        Plays 1497-1642.</u>   New York: Barnes and Noble,
        1963.   pp. 102-107.

103.   Jordan, John Clark.   <u>Robert Greene.</u>   pp. 187-189.

104.   Nelson, Malcolm A.   "The Sources of <u>George-a-
        Greene, The Pinner of Wakefield</u>," <u>PQ,</u> 42 (April
        1963), 159-165.

105.   Nicholson, B.   "Some Textual Remarks on the Play
        of <u>George-a-Greene,</u>" <u>N & Q,</u> 75 (January 29,
        1887), 81-82.

106.   Pennel, Charles A.   "The Authenticity of the <u>George-
        a-Greene</u> Title-Page Inscriptions," <u>JEGP,</u> 64
        (October 1965), 668-676.

107.   "<u>The Pinner of Wakefield</u> and Battell Bridge Field,"
        <u>N & Q,</u> 138 (April 17, 1920), 134-135.

108.   Sykes, H. Dugdale.   "Robert Greene and <u>George-a-
        Greene, the Pinner of Wakefield,</u>" <u>RES,</u> 7 (1931),
        129-136.

109.   Thomas, W. J. (ed.). "The History of George-a-
        Greene," Early English Prose Romances. London:
        Nattali and Bond, 1907. pp. 557-600.

110.   Whiting, G. W. "The Betrothal of Margaret and
        Lacy," TLS, November 6, 1930. p. 17.

        (7) Greene and Others (Comparative Studies)

111.   Acheson, Arthur. "Robert Greene's Collaboration
        with Lodge and Nashe," in his Shakespeare,
        Chapman and Sir Thomas More. New York:
        Edmond Byrne Hackett, 1931. pp. 135-183.

112.   Allen, P. "Shakespeare's Borrowings from Robert
        Greene," Shakespeare, Jonson and Wilkins as
        Borrowers. London: Palmer, 1928. pp. 32-35.

113.   Austin, W. B. "Supposed Contemporary Allusion to
        Shakespeare As a Plagiarist (Attack upon Shakes-
        peare in Greene's Groatsworth of Wits)," Shakes-
        peare Quarterly, 6 (Fall 1955), 373-380.

114.   Baildon, H. B. "Robert Greene and Titus and Andron-
        icus," in the Arden edition of the play. Cam-
        bridge: Harvard University Press, 1953. pp.
        lxx-lxxviii.

115.   Baker, G. P. "The Plays of the University Wits,"
        in CHEL, V, Chapter VI, p. 136.

116.   Baldwin, Thomas W. On the Literary Genetics of
        Shakespeare's Plays 1592-1594. Urbana: Univ-
        ersity of Illinois, 1959. Passim.

117.   Baskervill, C. R. English Elements in Jonson's
        Early Comedy. Austin: University of Texas
        Press, 1911. Passim.

118.   Bass, Eben. "Swinburne, Greene, and The Triumph
        of Time," Victorian Poetry, 4 (Winter 1966),
        56-61.

119.   Bentley, Gerald Eades. Shakespeare, a Biographical
        Handbook. New Haven: Yale University Press,
        1962, pp. 94-97 & passim.

120. Bond, R. Warwick. The Complete Works of John
      Lyly. 3 volumes. Oxford: Clarendon Press,
      1902. Passim.

121. Bovinski, Ludwig. "The Origin of the Euphuistic
      Novel and Its Significance of Shakespeare," in
      Studies in Honor of T. W. Baldwin. Urbana:
      University of Illinois Press, 1958. pp. 38-52.

122. Bradbrook, Muriel C. "Beasts and Gods: Greene's
      Groatsworth of Witte and the Social Purpose of
      Venus and Adonis," Shakespeare Survey, 15(1962),
      62-72.

123. Brooke, C. F. T. "The Green-Peele Myth," The
      Authorship of 2 and 3 Henry VI. New Haven:
      Yale University Press, 1912. pp. 188-194.

124. ----. "Was Greene the Original Author of 1 Henry
      VI?" in his edition of 1 Henry VI. New Haven:
      Yale University Press, 1918. pp. 150-151.

125. Brown, J. M. "An Early Rival of Shakespeare,"
      New Zealand Magazine, 6 (April 1877), 97-133.
      (* Reproduced substantially in Vol. I of Grosart's
      edition of Greene's works.)

126. Brown, John Russell, and Harris, Bernard (eds.).
      Early Shakespeare (Stratford-upon-Avon Studies,
      3). London: Arnold, 1961.

127. Butler, P. "Robert Greene," Materials for the Life
      of Shakespeare. Chapel Hill: University of North
      Carolina Press, 1930. pp. 55-60.

128. Camden, C. "Chaucer and Greene," RES, 6 (Jan-
      uary 1930), 73-74.

129. Cazamian, L. F. "Greene, Sidney, Peele," in his
      The Development of English Humor. New York:
      Macmillan, 1930. pp. 136-140.

130. Chapman, William Hall. William Shakespeare and
      Robert Greene. Oakland, California: Tribune
      Publishing Co. , 1912. pp. iv, 178.

131.   Clarkson, Paul S. and Warren, Clyde T. The Law
        of Property in Shakespeare and the Elizabethan
        Drama. Baltimore: Johns Hopkins University,
        1942. Passim.

132.   Cowl, R. P. "Robert Greene and Thomas Lodge,"
        Sources of the Text of Henry VI. Bruges: (n. p.),
        1928. pp. 12-14.

133.   Craig, Hardin. "Robert Greene," Shakespeare: A
        Historical and Critical Study. Chicago: (n. p.),
        1931. pp. 27-29; 82-87.

134.   Dent, Robert W. "Greene's Gwydonius: The Carde
        of Fancie: A Study in Elizabethan Plagiarism,"
        HLQ, 24 (1961), 151-152 [YWES, 42(1961), 155]
        Greene's Mamillia & Pettie's Peitie Pallace].

135.   De Perott, J. "Robert Greene and the Italian Trans-
        lation of Achilles Tatius," MLN, 29 (February
        1914), 63.

136.   Drake, N. "Robert Greene," Shakespeare and His
        Times. London: T. Cadell & W. Davies, 1817.
        I, 626-627; II, 249-251, 257-260.

137.   Drew, Philip. "Was Greene's Young Juvenal Nashe
        or Lodge?" Studies in English Literature, 1500-
        1900, 7 (Winter, 1967), 55-56.

138.   Ekelbald, Inga-stina. "King Lear and Selimus,"
        N & Q, 202 (May 1957), 193-194.

139.   Ellis-Fermor, Una M. "Marlowe and Greene: A
        Note on Their Relations as Dramatic Artists,"
        Studies in Honor of T. W. Baldwin. University of
        Illinois Press, 1958. pp. 136-149.

140.   Fleay, Frederick Gard. A Chronicle History of the
        Life and Work of William Shakespeare, Player,
        Poet, and Playmaker. London: J. C. Nimmo,
        1886. Passim.

141.   Forsythe, R. S. "Notes on The Spanish Tragedy,"
        Philological Quarterly, 5 (January 1926), 78-84.

142.   Gaw, Allison.   "The Origin and Development of 1
         Henry VI in Relation to Shakespeare, Marlowe,
         Peele, and Greene," University of Southern Cali-
         fornia Studies, Series I, No. 1. 1926.   80.

143.   Gosse, E.   Introduction to The Complete Works of
         Thomas Lodge.   4 volumes.   The Hunterian Club,
         1883.

144.   Graves, Thornton S.   "Some Chaucer Allusions,"
         SP, 27 (1930), 469-478.

145.   Gray, H. D.   "Greene as a Collaborator," MLN, 30
         (December 1915), 244-246.

146.   "Greene's Abuse of Shakespeare," Academy, 5 (April
         4, 1874), 368.

147.   Greg, W. W.   "(Giraldi) Cintio and the English
         Drama," MLQ, 3 (December 1900), 189-190;
         MLQ, 5 (July 1902), 72-73.

148.   Grosart, Alexander B. (ed.).   The Life and Com-
         plete Works in Prose and Verse of Robert Greene,
         M. A. in 15 volumes.   Volume I.   Strojenko's
         Life of Robert Greene with Introduction and Notes.
         London: Privately printed, 1881-86.   pp. 227-256.

149.   ----.   "Was Robert Greene Substantially the Author
         of Titus Andronicus?" ES, 22 (1896), 389-436.

150.   Grundy, Joan.   "Shakespeare's Sonnets and the
         Elizabethan Sonneteers," Shakespeare Survey, 15
         (1962), 41-49 [YWES, 43 (1962), 125].

151.   Harrison G. B. (ed.).   Elizabethan and Jacobean
         Quartos: Thomas Nashe, Pierce Penilesse, His
         Svpplication to the Divell (1592).   New York:
         Barnes & Noble, 1966 (c. 1922).   p. viii.

152.   ----.   Shakespeare's Fellows.   London: John Lane,
         1923.

153.   Harvey, Gabriel.   "From Foure Letters, (1592), in
         Elizabethan Critical Essays, ed.   G. G. Smith
         (ed.).   Oxford: Clarendon Press, 1904.   II,
         229-238.

154.   Hayashi, Tetsumaro. "Controversy Between Gosson
       and Lodge," Lumina, XII (1969), 75-79.

155.   Holzknecht, Karl J.   The Backgrounds of Shakes-
       peare's Plays. New York: American Book Co.,
       1950. Passim.

156.   Honk, R. A. "Shakespeare's Shrew and Greene's
       Orlando," PMLA, 62 (September 1947), 657-671.

157.   Jordan, J. C. "Robert Greene and George Gascoigne,"
       MLN, 30 (February 1915), 61-62.

158.   J. P. "Robert Greene and Gabriel Harvey," N & Q,
       16 (October 24, 1857), 324-325.

159.   Kennedy, H. A. "Greene's Criticism of Shakespeare,"
       N & Q, 45 (March 23, 1872), 237.

160.   Kettner, Eugene J. "Love's Labour's Lost and the
       Harvey-Nashe-Greene Quarrel," Emporia State
       Research Studies, 10 (1962), 29-39.

161.   Landt, D. B. "The Ancestry of Sir John Falstaff,"
       Shakespeare Quarterly, 17 (Winter 1966), 69-76.

162.   Law, Robert A.   "Pre-Conceived Pattern of A
       Midsummer Night's Dream," University of Texas
       Studies in English (1943), pp. 5-14.

163.   Livesay, John L. "Robert Greene, Master of Arts,
       and Mayster Guazzo," SP, 36 (October 1939),
       577-596.

164.   McGinn, Donald J. "A Quip from Tom Nashe," in
       Studies in the English Renaissance Drama, ed.
       Josephine W. Bennett, et al (eds.). New York:
       New York University Press, 1959. pp. 172-188.

165.   McNeal, Thomas H. "Who Is Silvia?-- and Other
       Problems in the Greene-Shakespeare Relationship,"
       Shakespeare Association Bulletin, 13 (1938), 240-
       254.

166.   McNeir, Waldo F. "Greene's Tomliuclin: Tambur-
       laine, or Tom a Lincoln?" MLN, 58 (May 1943),
       380-382.

167.   ----. "Heywood's Source, for the Main Plot of A
        Woman Killed with Kindness," in Studies in the
        English Renaissance Drama, ed. by Josephine
        W. Bennett, et al (eds.). New York University
        Press, 1959. pp. 189-211.

168.   ----. "Reconstructing the Conclusion of John of
        Bordeau (Attributed to Greene)," PMLA, 66 (June
        1951), 540-543.

169.   ----. "Robert Greene and John of Bordeaux,"
        PMLA, 64 (September 1949), 781-801.

170.   Marder, Louis. "Greene's Attack on Shakespeare:
        A Posthumous Hoax?" SNL, 16 (September 1966),
        29-30.

171.   Miller, Edwin H. "Relationship of Robert Greene
        and Thomas Nashe (1588-1592)," PQ, 33 (October
        1954), 353-367.

172.   ----. "Robert Parsons' Resolution and The Repen-
        tance of Robert Greene," N & Q, 199 (March
        1954), 104-108.

173.   ----. "Samuel Rid's Borrowings from Robert
        Greene," N & Q, 199 (June 1954), 236-238.

174.   Muir, Kenneth. "Greene and Troilus and Cressida,"
        N & Q, 200 (April 1955), 141-142.

175.   Murphy, D. "Shakespeare's Debt to Robert Greene,"
        Irish Monthly Magazine, 42 (September 1934),
        555-557.

176.   Norman, Charles. So Worthy a Friend: William
        Shakespeare. New York: Collier Books, 1961.
        Passim.

177.   Oliphant, E. H. (ed.). Shakespeare and His Fellow
        Dramatists. New York: Prentice-Hall, 1929.

178.   Pafford, J. H. P. (ed.). The Winter's Tale (The
        Arden Shakespeare) Harvard University Press,
        1962 [YWES, 44 (1963), 125-126] (Greene's
        Pandosto).

179. Paradise, N. Burton. Thomas Lodge: The History
      of an Elizabethan. New Haven: Yale University
      Press, 1931.

180. Parr, Johnstone. "Robert Greene and His Class-
      mates at Cambridge," PMLA, 77 (1962), 536-
      543.

181. Pennel, Charles A. "Robert Greene and King or
      Kaisar," ELN, 3 (1965) 24-26.
      (* Phrase supports Greene's Authorship of George
      a-Greene).

182. Ribner, Irving. "Greene's Attack on Marlowe:
      Some Light on Alphonsus and Selimus," SP, 52
      (April 1955), 162-171.

183. Robertson, John M. Marlowe: A Conspectus.
      London: [n. p.], 1931. Passim.

184. ----. Did Shakespeare Write Titus Andronicus?
      London: Watts, 1905. pp. 141-175.

185. ----. Introduction to the Study of The Shakespeare
      Canon. London: Routledge, 1924.

186. ----. The Shakespeare Canon. London: Routledge,
      I, 1922; II, 1923; III, 1925; IV, 1930.

187. ----. The State of Shakespeare Study. London:
      Routledge, 1931. Passim.

188. Rowse, A. L. William Shakespeare: A Biography.
      New York: Pocket Books, 1965 [c. 1963]. Pas-
      sim.

189. Sanders, Norman. "The Comedy of Greene and
      Shakespeare," Early Shakespeare eds.   John
      Russell Brown & Bernard Harris.   Stratford-
      upon-Avon Series III.   New York: St. Martin's
      Press, 1962. pp. 35-53.

190. Saunders, Chauncey Elwood. "Robert Greene and
      His Editors," PMLA, 48 (1933), 392-417.

191. Schrickx, W. "Nashe, Greene, and Shakespeare in
      1592," Revue des Langues Vivantes (Brussels),

I (1956), 55-64.

192.   ----. Shakespeare's Early Contemporaries. Ant-
       werpen, Nederlandische Bolkhandel, 1956. Pas-
       sim.

193.   Secombe, Thomas and Allen, J. W. The Age of
       Shakespeare. London: Bell, 1911. 2 volumes.
       Passim.

194.   Simpson, Richard. "Greene on Nashe," Academy,
       5 (April 11, 1874), 400 and passim.
       (* Also "Chettle on Shakespeare," The School of
       Shakespeare, by David L. Frost. Cambridge,
       England: University Press, 1968. II, 330.)

195.   ----. "Greene on Nashe; on Marlowe; and on Shake-
       speare," Shakespeare Allusion Book. ed. by
       C. M. Ingleby (ed.). Part I, passim.

196.   Sisson, Charles J. (ed.). Thomas Lodge and Other
       Elizabethans. Cambridge: Harvard University
       Press, 1933.

197.   Smart, J. S. "Robert Greene and Shakespeare,"
       Shakespeare Truth and Tradition. London: E.
       Arnold & Co., pp. 107-109; 191-199.

198.   Smith, F. A. "Robert Greene," The Critics vs.
       Shakespeare. New York: Knickerbocker Press,
       1907. Passim.

199.   Smith, G. C. M. "Lyly, Greene, and Shakespeare,"
       N & Q, 116 (December 14, 1907), 461.

200.   South, Helen P. "The Upstart Crow," MP, 25
       (1927), 83-86.

201.   Spens, J. "Greene's Influence on Shakespeare,"
       Essay on Shakespeare's Relation to Tradition.
       Oxford: B. H. Blackwell, 1916. pp. 13-15.

202.   Staunton, H. "A Mistaken Allusion to Shakespeare,"
       Athenaeum, No. 2415 (February 7, 1874), 193.

203.   "Suppositions about Shakespeare," New Monthly Mag-
       azine, 60 (November 1840), 297-304.

204.   Swinburne, A. C. "Marlowe in Relation to Robert
        Greene, George Peele, and Thomas Lodge,"
        Contemporaries of Shakespeare. London: Heine-
        mann, 1919. pp. 1-12.

205.   Sykes, H. D. "Robert Greene and King Leir,"
        Sidelights on Shakespeare. Stratford, England:
        Shakespeare Head Press, pp. 141-142.

206.   Symonds, John A. Shakespeare's Predecessors in
        the English Drama. London: Smith, Elder, and
        Co. , 1900.

207.   Talbert, Ernest W. Elizabethan Drama and Shake-
        speare's Early Plays. Chapel Hill: University
        of North Carolina Press, 1963. Passim.

208.   Thomas, Sidney. "The Meaning of Greene's Attack
        on Shakespeare," MLN, 66 (November 1951),
        483-484.

209.   Tonybee, Paget. "Two Alleged Quotations from
        Dante," Athenaeum, 1 (Fall 15, 1902), 210.

210.   ----. "References to Dante," Athenaeum, No. 3877
        (February 15, 1902), 216.

211.   Tynan, J. L. "Influence of Greene on Shakespeare's
        Early Romance," PMLA, 27 (June 1912), 246-
        264.

212.   Vincent, C. J. "Pettie and Greene," MLN, 54 (Fall
        1939), 105-111.

213.   Walker, Roy. " 'The Upstart Crow'," TLS, August
        10, 1951. p. 501.

214.   Wells, Stanley W. "Greene and Pliny," N & Q, 206
        (November 1961), 422-424 [YWES, 42(1961), 155].

215.   Wright, Celeste Turner. "Munday and Chettle in
        Grub Street," Boston University Studies in Eng-
        lish, 5 (Autumn 1961), 129-138.

216.   Wynne, Arnold. "Comedy: Lyly, Greene, Peele,
        Nash," in the Growth of English Drama. Oxford:
        Clarendon Press, 1914. pp. 124-192.

(8) Groatsworth of Wit (Romance, 1592)

217.   Austin, Warren B.   "The Posthumous Greene Pam-
        phlets: A Computerized Study," SNL, 16 (Nov-Dec.
        1966), 45.

218.   ----. "Supposed Contemporary Allusion to Shake-
        speare As a Plagiarist," Shakespeare Quarterly,
        6 (Fall 1955), 373-380.

219.   Baldwin, Thomas W.   On the Literary Genetics of
        Shakespeare's Plays 1592-1594.   Urbana: Univ-
        ersity of Illinois, 1959. pp. 1-55.

220.   Bradbrook, Muriel C.   "Beasts and Gods: Greene's
        Groatsworth of Witte and the Social Purpose of
        Venus and Adonis," Shakespeare Survey, 15 (1962),
        62-72.

221.   Brown, J. M.   "An Early Rival of Shakespeare,"
        New Zealand Magazine, 2 (April 1877), 97-133.

222.   Chapman, William Hall.   "Who Was Shake-scene?"
        Shakespeare The Personal Phase.   Los Angeles:
        United Printing Co. , 1920.   pp. 281-371.

223.   Corser, T.   "Greene's Groatsworth of Witte," N &
        Q, 3 (June 14, 1851), 479.

224.   Day, Martin S.   History of English Literature to
        1660.   Garden City, N. Y. : Doubleday, 1963.
        Passim.

225.   Drew, Philip.   "Was Greene's Young Juvenal Nashe
        or Lodge?" Studies in English Literature, 1500-
        1900, 7 (Winter 1967), 55-66.

226.   Jenkins, Harold.   "On the Authenticity of Greene's
        Groatsworth of Wit and The Repentance of Robert
        Greene," RES, 11 (1935), 28-41.

227.   Jordan, John Clark.   Robert Greene.   pp. 62-65.

228.   NcNeal, T. H.   "Problems in the Robert Greene-
        Shakespeare Relationship," Shakespeare Association
        Bulletin, 13 (October 1938), 240-245.

229.   ----. "The Tygers Heart Wrapped in a Player's
        Hide," Shakespeare Association Bulletin, 13 (Jan-
        uary 1938), 30-39.

230.   Marder, Louis. "Greene's Attack on Shakespeare:
        A Posthumous Hoax?" SNL, 16 (September 1966),
        29-30.

231.   Schelling, F. E. "The Groatsworth of Wit," in his
        Queene's Progress and Other Elizabethan Sketches.
        Boston: Houghton, Mifflin, 1904. pp. 131-147.

232.   South, Helen P. "The Upstart Crow," MP, 25
        (1927), 83-86.

233.   Squire, Sir John Collings. "Greenes Groatsworth
        of Witte" in Books in General ed. by Solomon
        Eagle. New York: Knopf, 1920. pp. 157-162.

234.   Theobald, R. M. "The Groatsworth of Wit," in
        Shakespeare Studies in Baconian Light. London:
        Low, Marston, 1901. pp. 13-16

235.   Thomas, Sidney. "The Meaning of Greene's Attack
        on Shakespeare," MLN, 66 (November 1951), 483-
        484.

236.   Walker, Roy. " 'The Upstart Crow'," TLS, August
        10, 1951. p. 501.

(9) James IV (Play, 1598)

237.   Brooke, C. F. Tucker. The Tudor Drama: Hamden,
        Conn.: Archon Books, 1964 [c. 1911]. pp. 266-
        268.

238.   Chambers, E. K. The Elizabethan Stage. 4 volumes.
        Oxford: Clarendon Press, 1961. II, 296; III,
        330.

239.   Collins, J. Churton (ed.). The Plays and Poems of
        Robert Greene. Oxford: Clarendon Press, 1905.
        II, 79-85.

240.   Ellis-Fermor, Una. "Marlowe and Greene: A Note
        on Their Relationship as Dramatic Artists," in
        Studies in Honor of T. W. Baldwin. Urbana:

University of Illinois Press, 1958. pp. 136-149.

241. Gayley, Charles Mills. Representative English Com-
      edies. New York: Macmillan, 1930. I, 415-
      418.

242. Holzknecht, Karl J. Outlines of Tudor and Stuart
      Plays 1947-1642. New York: Barnes and Noble,
      1963. pp. 112-118.

243. Hudson, Ruth. "Greene's James IV and Contemporary
      Allusions to Scotland," PMLA, 47 (September
      1932), 652-667.

244. Jordan, John Clark. Robert Greene. pp. 181-182;
      190-197.

245. MacLaine, A. H. "Greene's Borrowings from His
      Own Prose Fiction in Bacon and Bungay and
      James IV," PQ. 30 (January 1951), 22-29.

246. McNeir, Waldo F. "The Original of Ateukin in
      Greene's James IV," MLN, 42 (June 1947), 376-
      381.

247. Manley, John Matthews. Specimens of the Pre-
      Shakespearean Drama. Boston: Ginn, 1897.
      Vol. II, pp. 327-418.

248. Muir, Kenneth. "Robert Greene as Dramatist," in
      Essays on Shakespeare and Elizabethan Drama in
      Honor of Hardin Craig. pp. 51-54.

249. Tannenbaum, S. A. "A Forgery in a Copy of James
      IV," Shakespearean Scraps and Other Elizabethan
      Fragments. New York: Columbia University
      Press, 1933, pp. 49-50.

250. Van Dam, B. A. P. "Greene's James IV," English
      Studies, 14 (1932), 97-122.

      (10) A Looking Glasse For London and England
           With Thomas Lodge (Play, 1594)

251. Acheson, Arthur. "Robert Greene's Collaboration
      with Lodge and Nashe," in his Shakespeare,
      Chapman and Sir Thomas More. New York:

Edmond Byrne Hackett, 1931. pp. 135-183.

252.   Baskerville, Charles Read. "A Prompt Copy of A
       Looking Glass for London and England," MP, 30
       (August 1932), 29-51.

253.   Brooke, C. F. Tucker. The Tudor Drama. Hamden,
       Conn.: Archon Books, 1964 [c. 1911]. p. 246.

254.   Bubb, Laurence. The Elizabethan Malady: A Study
       of Melancholia in Elizabethan Literature from
       1580 to 1640. East Lansing: Michigan State
       College Press, 1951. pp. 119+.

255.   Chambers, E. K. The Elizabethan Stage. III, p.
       328, passim.

256.   Clugston, George Alan. "A Looking Glasse for
       London and England, By Thomas Lodge and Robert
       Greene. A Critical Edition," Unpublished Ph. D.
       dissertation, University of Michigan, 1967.

257.   Collins, J. Churton (ed.). The Plays and Poems of
       Robert Greene. Oxford: Clarendon Press, 1905.
       I, 137-142.

258.   Cotham, Margaret Mary. "Greene and Lodge's A
       Looking Glass for London and England," Unpub-
       lished M. A. thesis, University of Texas, 1928.

259.   Ford, Boris (ed.). The Age of Shakespeare. Balti-
       more: Penguin Books, 1962. pp. 57-59.

260.   Gayley, Charles Mills. Representative English
       Comedies. New York: Macmillan, 1930.   I,
       406-408.

261.   Greene, H. W. "An Emendation in A Looking Glass,"
       TLS, March 13, 1924. p. 160.

262.   Harrison, G. B. Elizabethan Plays and Players.
       Ann Arbor: University of Michigan Press, 1961.
       86-90.

263.   Hayashi, Tetsumaro. "An Edition of A Looking
       Glasse for London and England by Thomas Lodge
       and Robert Greene," Unpublished Ph. D. disser-

tation, Kent State University, 1968.

264.   ----. A Textual Study of A Looking Glasse for Lon-
        don and England By Thomas Lodge and Robert
        Greene. Muncie, Indiana: Ball State University,
        1969 [BSU Monograph Series].

265.   Homan, Sidney R. "A Looking-glass for London and
        England: The Source for Dekker's If It Be Not
        a Play, The Devil Is in It," N & Q, 211 (August
        1966), 301-302.

266.   Jordan, John Clark. Robert Greene. pp. 177-179.

267.   Law, Robert A. "A Looking Glasse and the Scrip-
        tures," University of Texas Studies in English,
        1939. pp. 31-47.

268.   ----. "Two Parallels to Greene and Lodge's Look-
        ing-glass," MLN, 26 (May 1911), 146-148.

269.   McNeir, Waldo F. "The Date of A Looking Glass
        for London," N & Q, 200 (July 1955), 282-283.

270.   Muir, Kenneth. "Robert Greene as Dramatist," in
        Essays on Shakespeare and Elizabethan Drama in
        Honor of Hardin Craig. p. 47+.

271.   Paradise, N. Burton. Thomas Lodge: The History
        of an Elizabethan. New Haven: Yale University
        Press, 1931. pp. 142-157; passim.

272.   Rae, Wesley D. Thomas Lodge. New York: Twayne,
        1967. pp. 43-44.

273.   Roston, Murray. Biblical Drama in England from
        Middle Ages to the Present Day. Evanston:
        Northwestern University Press, 1968. Passim.

274.   Schelling, Felix E. Elizabethan Drama 1558-1642.
        Boston: Houghton, Mifflin, 1908. I, 41, 241-242.

275.   Swaen, A. E. H. "A Looking-glass for London and
        England: Nutmegs and Ginger," MLR, 33 (July
        1938), 404-405.

276.   Walker, A.   "Greg's Edition of A Looking-glass,"
        RES, 10 (April 1934), 223-225.

        (11) A Maidens Dreame (Poem, 1591)

277.   Collins, J. Churton (ed.).   The Plays and Poems of
        Robert Greene.   II, 219-220.

278.   Jordan, John Clark.   Robert Greene.   Passim.

279.   McMillan, Mary Evelyn.   "An Edition of Greenes
        Vision and A Maidens Dreame By Robert Greene,"
        Unpublished Ph. D. dissertation, University of
        Alabama, 1960.

        (12) Mamillia (Romance, I, 1583; II, 1593)

280.   Dent, Robert W.   "Greene's Gwydonius: The Carde
        of Francie: A Study in Elizabethan Plagiarism,"
        HLQ, 24 (1961), 151-162 [Mamillia and Pettie's
        Petite Pallace].

281.   Hornat, Jaroslav.   "Mamillia: Robert Greene's Con-
        troversy with Euphues," Philological Pragensia, 5
        (1962), 210-218 [YWES, 44 (1963), 192].

282.   Jordan, John Clark.   Robert Greene.   Passim.

        (13) Menaphon (Romance, 1589)

283.   Adams, J. Q.   "Greene's Menaphon and the Thracian
        Wonder," MP, 3 (January 1906), 317-325.

284.   Berereton, J. LeGay.   "The Relation of The Thracian
        Wonder to Greene's Menaphon," MLR, 2 (October
        1906), 34-38.

285.   Hill, N. W.   "On Greene's Menaphon," N & Q, 118
        (August 1, 1908), 85-86.

286.   Jordan, John Clark.   Robert Greene.   pp. 39-42.

287.   Knapp, M.   "A Note on Nashe's Preface to Greene's
        Menaphon," N & Q, 164 (February 11, 1933), 98.

288.   Quaintance, Richard E., Jr.   "The French Source of
        Robert Greene's 'What Thing Is Love'," N & Q,

208 (August 1963), 295-296 [YWES, 44 (1963),
189].

289.   Smith, G. G. (ed.). "Nashe's Preface to Menaphon,"
       Elizabethan Critical Essays, Oxford: Clarendon
       Press, 1904.   I, 307-320; 423-428.

290.   Strojenko, Nicholas.   "The Date of Greene's Mena-
       phon," N & Q, 48 (December 6, 1873), 441-442.

(14) Orlando Furioso (Play, 1594)

291.   Bradbrook, M. C.   The Growth and Structure of
       Elizabethan Comedy.   Baltimore: Penguin Books,
       1963 [c. 1955].   pp. 77-78.

292.   Brooke, C. F. Tucker.   The Tudor Drama.   Hamden,
       Conn.: Archon Books, 1964 [c. 1911] p. 246.

293.   Chambers, E. K.   The Elizabethan Stage.   I, 378;
       II, 268; III, 325, 329, 461, 472.

294.   Collins, J. Churton (ed.).   The Plays and Poems of
       Robert Greene.   I, 215-219.

295.   Gayley, Charles Mills.   Representative English Com-
       edies.   I, 408-411.

296.   Heipich, C. A.   "A Parallel Between Greene's Or-
       lando and Marlowe's Dido," N & Q, 114 (Septem-
       ber 8, 1906), 185.

297.   Honk, R. A. "Shakespeare's Shrew and Greene's
       Orlando," PMLA, 62 (September 1947), 657-671.

298.   Jordan, John Clark.   Robert Greene. pp. 179-180,
       193-195.

299.   Lemmi, C. W.   "The Sources of Orlando Furioso,"
       MLN, 31 (November 1916), 440-441.

300.   McNeir, Waldo F.   "Source of Simon Eyre's Catch-
       Phrase; Greene's Orlando Furioso," MLN, 53
       (April 1938), 257-276.

301.   Morrison, Morris R.   "Greene's Use of Ariosto in
       Orlando Furioso," MLN, 49 (November 1934),

449-451.

302. Muir, Kenneth. "Robert Greene as Dramatist," in
Essays on Shakespeare and Elizabethan Drama in
Honor of Hardin Craig. p. 47.

303. Mukherjee, Sujit Kumar. "The Text of Greene's
Orlando Furioso," Indian Journal of English
Studies (1965), 102-107.

304. Peers, E. A. "Orlando Furioso," Elizabethan
Drama and Its Mad Folk. Cambridge: W. Heffer,
1914. Passim.

305. Shackford, H. "As You Like It and Orlando Furioso,"
MLN, 39 (January 1924), 54-56.

306. Soellner, Rolf. "The Madness of Hercules and the
Elizabethans," Comparative Literature, 10 (Fall
1958), 309-324.

307. Van Dam, B. A. P. "Alleyn's Player's Part of Orlando Furioso and the 1594 Text," English Studies,
11(October 1929), 182-203; (December 1929), 209-
220.

(15) Pandosto (Romance, 1588)

308. Brandes, G. (ed.). "Pandosto and The Winter's
Tale," in his edition of Shakespeare's The Winter's
Tale. New York: 1905. pp. v-ix.

309. Delius, N. "Greene's Pandosto and The Winter's
Tale," Shakespeare Jahrbuch, 15 (1880), 22-43.

310. Jordan, John Clark. Robert Greene. pp. 37-39.

311. Kozmian, Stanislaus. "A Winter's Tale," Athenaeum,
6 (1875), 609.

312. Lawlor, John. "Pandosto and the Nature of Dramatic
Romance," PQ, 41 (January 1962), 96-113.

313. McNeal, Thomas H. "Clerk's Tale as a Possible
Source for Pandosto," PMLA, 47 (June 1932),
453-460.

314. Moorman, F. W. "Pandosto and The Winter's Tale,"
     in his introduction to the Arden Edition of the
     play. London: (n. p.), 1912.

315. Morley, H. (ed.). "Pandosto, in his Shorter Works
     in English Prose. London: (n. p.), (n. d.). pp.
     49-65.

316. Nicholson, W. "Pandosto and The Winter's Tale,"
     MLN, 21 (November 1906), 219-220.

317. Pafford, J. H. P. (ed.). The Winter's Tale (The
     Arden Shakespeare): Harvard University Press,
     1963 [YWES, 44 (1963), 125-126].

318. Pierce, F. E. "Pandosto and The Winter's Tale," in
     his edition of The Winter's Tale. New Haven:
     Yale University Press, 1918. pp. 128-130.

319. Porter, C. and Clarke, H. A. (eds.). "Pandosto and
     The Winter's Tale," in their First Folio edition
     of the play. New York: T. Y. Crowell, 1908.
     pp. 118-125.

320. Quiller-Couch, A. "Pandosto and The Winter's
     Tale," in the new Cambridge edition of the play.
     Cambridge: University Press, 1931. pp. xiii-
     xviii.

321. Thomas, P. G. (ed.). "Pandosto, a Review," Book-
     man (London), 34 (June 1908), 112-113.

322. Weld, J. S. "W. Bettie's Titana and Theseus and
     His Borrowings from Greene's Pandosto," PQ,
     26 (January 1947), 36-44.

323. Wells, Stanley. "Some Words in 1588: Perymedes
     The Blacksmith and Pandosto," N & Q, 207
     (June 1962), 205-207.

(16) Penelope's Web (Romance, 1587)

324. Bratchell, D. F. "An Edition of the Planetomachia
     and Penelope's Web of Robert Greene," Unpublished
     Ph. D. dissertation, University of Birmingham,
     1955-56. [Index, VI:9].

325.   McNeir, Waldo F.   "A Proverb of Greene's Emended
        Penelope's Web," N & Q, 197 (March 1952), 117.

        (17) Philomela (Romance, 1592)

326.   Dean, James S., Jr.   "Antedatings from Robert
        Greene," N & Q, 208 (August 1963), 297-298.

327.   ----.   "Borrowings from Robert Greene's Philo-
        mela in Robert Davenport's The City-Night-Cap,"
        N & Q, 211 (August 1966), 302-303.

328.   Jordan, J. C.   "Davenport's The City Nightcap and
        Greene's Philomela," MLN, 36 (May 1921), 281-
        284.

        (18) Planetomachia (Romance, 1585)

329.   Bratchell, D. F.   "An Edition of the Planetomachia
        and Penelope's Web of Robert Greene," Unpub-
        lished Ph. D. dissertation, University of Birming-
        ham, 1955-56.   [Index, VI:9].

330.   Bubb, Laurence.   The Elizabethan Malady: A Study
        of Melancholia in Elizabethan Literature from
        1580 to 1640.   East Lansing: Michigan State
        College Press, 1951.   pp. 88-89.

331.   Parr, Johnstone.   "Sources of the Astrological Pre-
        faces in Robert Greene's Planetomachia," SP,
        46 (July 1949), 400-410.

332.   "Planetomachia (1585)," TLS, August 24, 1916.   p.
        405.   December 21, p. 625; January 15, 1920.   p.
        36.

333.   Saunders, C. and Jackson, W. A.   "Note on Robert
        Greene's Planetomachia, 1585," Library, 54 (March
        1936), 444-447.

        (19) A Quip for An Upstart Courtier
        (Repentance Pamphlet, 1592)

334.   Harrison, G. B. (ed.).   Elizabethan and Jacobean
        Quartos: Thomas Nashe, Pierce, Penilesse, His
        Svpllication to the Divell (1592).   New York:
        Barnes & Noble, 1966 (c. 1922).   p. viii.

335.   Jordan, John Clark. Robert Greene. pp. 121-126.

336.   McGinn, Donald J. "A Quip from Tom Nashe," in
       Studies in The English Renaissance Drama, ed.
       by Josephine W. Bennett, et al (eds.). New York:
       University Press, 1959. pp. 172-188.

337.   Miller, Edwin H. (ed.). Ciceronis Amor: Tullies
       Love and A Quip for an Upstart Courtier (1592).
       Gainsville, Florida: Scholars' Facsimile and
       Reprints, 1954 [YWES, 36 (1955), 140].

338.   ----. "Deletion in Robert Greene's A Quip for an
       Upstart Courtier (1592)," HLQ, 15 (May 1952),
       277-282.

339.   ----. "The Editions of Robert Greene's A Quip for
       an Upstart Courtier (1592)," SB, 6 (1953), 107-
       116 [YWES, 35 (1954), 247].

340.   ----. "The Sources of Robert Greene's A Quip for
       an Upstart Courtier (1592)," N & Q, 198 (April
       1953), 148-152. Also in 198 (May 1953), 187-
       191 [YWES, 34 (1953), 181].

341.   Nathanson, Leonard. "A Quip for an Upstart Court-
       ier and The Three Ladies of London," N & Q,
       201 (1956), 376-377 [YWES, 37 (1956), 143].

342.   Oldys, W. And Park, T. (eds.). "A Quip for an
       Upstart Courtier" in Harleian Miscellany. London:
       Oxford Press, 1810. V, 393-421.

343.   Parker, R. B. "Alteration in the First Edition of
       Greene's A Quip for an Upstart Courtier (1592),"
       HLQ, 23 (February 1960), 181-186 [YWES, 41
       (1960), 144].

344.   ----. "A Dutch Edition of Robert Greene's A Quip
       for an Upstart Courtier (1601)," N & Q, 205
       (April 1960), 130-134 [YWES, 41 (1960), 144].

345.   Shapiro, I. A. "The First Edition of Greene's Quip
       for an Upstart Courtier," Studies in Bibliography,
       14 (1961), 212-218 [YWES, 42(1961), 25].

(20) The Repentance (Repentance Pamphlet, 1592)

346.   Austin, Warren B. "The Posthumous Greene Pam-
        phlets: A Computerized Study," SNL, 16 (Novem-
        ber-December 1966), 45.

347.   Jenkins, H. "On the Authorship of The Groatsworth
        of Wit and The Repentance of Robert Greene,"
        RES, 11 (January 1935), 28-41.

348.   Jordan, John Clark. Robert Greene. pp. 76-79.

349.   Miller, Edwin H. "Robert Parsons's Resolution
        and The Repentance of Robert Greene," N & Q,
        199 (March 1954), 104-108 [YWES, 35 (1954), 125].

350.   "The Repentance of Robert Greene," Book Lore, 4
        (December 1886), 10-14.

(21) Selimus (Play, 1594)

351.   Chambers, E. K. The Elizabethan Stage. IV, 27,
        46.

352.   Crawford, Chas. Collectanea. First Series, 1906.
        (Edmund Spenser's Locrine and Selimus.)

353.   ----. "Spenser's Locrine and Selimus," N & Q,
        104 (1901), 61-63; 101-103; 142-144; 203-205;
        260-261; 324-325; 384-386.

354.   Cunliffe, J. W. "Locrine and Selimus," CHEL, V,
        84-88+.

355.   Ekelbald, Inga-stina. "King Lear and Selimus,"
        N & Q, 202 (May 1957), 193-194.

356.   Gayley, Charles Mills. Representative English
        Comedies. New York: Macmillan, 1930. I,
        421-422.

357.   Grosart, A. (ed.). "Tragical Reign of Selimus.
        A Review," Athenaeum, 112 (August 27, 1898),
        299.

358.   Hubbard, F. G.   "Locrine and Selimus," Shakespeare
       Studies, Madison: University of Wisconsin Press,
       1916.   pp. 17-35.

359.   Jordan, John Clark.   Robert Greene.   pp. 184-186.

360.   Koeppel, E.   "Locrine and Selimus," Shakespeare
       Jahrbuch, 41 (1905), 193-200.

361.   Ribner, Irving.   "Greene's Attack on Marlowe:
       Some Light on Alphonsus and Selimus," SP, 52
       (1955), 162-171 [See YWES, 36 (1955), 129].

(22) The Spanish Masquerado (Romance, 1589)

362.   Curtis, G. B.   "A Study in Elizabethan Typography:
       A Cipher in The Spanish Masquerado," Baconiana,
       24 (January 1939), 6-12.

363.   Oliver, Leslie M.   "The Spanish Masquerado: A
       Problem in Double Edition," Library, 2 (June
       1947), 14-19.

(23) Vision (Romance-Repentance Pamphlet, 1592)

364.   Hayashi, Tetsumaro.   A Textual Study of A Looking
       Glasse for London and England By Thomas Lodge
       and Robert Greene.   Muncie, Indiana: Ball
       State University, 1969 [BSU Monograph Series],
       Passim.

365.   McMillan, Mary Evelyn.   "An Edition of Greenes
       Vision and A Maidens Dreame By Robert Greene,"
       Unpublished Ph. D. dissertation, University of
       Alabama, 1960.

366.   McNeir, Waldo F.   "The Date of Greene's Vision,"
       N & Q, 195 (April 1950), 137.

(24) Robert Greene As A Dramatist

367.   Black, Matthew.   "Enter Critizens," In Studies in
       the English Renaissance Drama ed. Josephine
       W. Bennett, et al.   New York: New York Univer-
       sity Press, 1959.   pp. 16-27.

368. Bluestone, Max.   "A Digest of a Review of Wolfgang
      Clemen's English Tragedy Before Shakespeare tr.
      by T. S. Dorsch.   London: Methuen, 1961; by
      Ralph Lawrence, English, 13 (1961), 235-236;
      in SNL, 12 (May 1962), 20.

369. Buland, M.   "Time in the Plays of Robert Greene,"
      The Presentation of Time in the Elizabethan
      Drama.   New York: H. Holt, 1912.   76-79; 239-
      257.

370. Busby, Olive Mary.   Studies in the Development of
      the Fool in the Elizabethan Drama.   London:
      Oxford University Press, 1923.

371. Chambers, E. K.   The Elizabethan Stage.   Passim.

372. Clemens, Wolfgang.   English Tragedy Before Shake-
      speare.   tr. by T. S. Dorsch.   London: Metaven,
      1961, passim.

373. Cunliffe, J. W.   "Early English Tragedy," CHEL,
      V, Chapter IV, p. 68.

374. ----.   "Robert Greene,"   The Influence of Seneca
      on Elizabethan Tragedy.   New York: Macmillan,
      1925.   pp. 62-66.

375. Ellis-Fermor, Una.   "Marlowe and Greene: A
      Note on Their Relationship as Dramatic Artists,"
      in Studies in Honor of T. W. Baldwin.   Urbana:
      University of Illinois Press, 1958.   pp. 136-149.

376. Empson, William.   "The Function of the Double
      Plot," in Shakespeare's Contemporaries, ed. Max
      Bluestone and Norman Rabkin.   pp. 31-35.
      [Originally in his Some Versions of Pastoral.
      London: Chatto & Windus, 1935.   pp. 27-34.

377. Fleay, F. G.   "Dates of Greene's Plays," Shakespeare
      Manual.   London: Macmillan, 1876.   pp. 286-
      295.

378. Gerrard, E. A.   "Robert Greene's Romantic Inter-
      ludes," Elizabethan Drama.   Oxford: Clarendon
      Press, 1928.   pp. 198-210.

379.   Grosart, Alexander B. (ed.).   The Life and Complete
       Works in Prose and Verse of Robert Greene, M. A.
       Volume I: Strojenko's Life of Robert Green With
       Introduction and Notes.   pp. 167-226.

380.   Harrison, G. B.   Elizabethan Plays and Players.
       Ann Arbor: University of Michigan Press, 1961.
       pp. 57-116.

381.   Hayashi, Tetsumaro.   A Textual Study of A Looking
       Glasse of London and England By Thomas Lodge
       and Robert Greene.   Muncie, Indiana: Ball State
       University, 1969 [BSU Monograph Series].   Passim.

382.   Johnson, W. N.   "The Devil as a Character in Lit-
       erature," Manchester Quarterly, 31 (1912), 324-
       341.

383.   Klein, David.   The Elizabethan Dramatists as
       Critics.   New York: Philosophical Library.   1963.
       Passim.

384.   Muir, Kenneth.   "Robert Greene as Dramatist," in
       Essays on Shakespeare and Elizabethan Drama
       in Honor of Hardin Craig, ed.   Richard Hosley.
       pp. 45-54.

385.   Mustard, W. P.   "Notes on Greene's Plays," MLN,
       40 (May 1925), 316-317.

386.   Oras, Ants.   Pause Patterns in Elizabethan and
       Jacobean Drama: An Experiment in Prosody.
       Gainesville, Florida: University of Florida Press,
       1963.   (* University of Florida Monographs,
       Humanities, No. 3, Winter, 1960).

387.   Parrott, Thomas Marc, and Ball, Robert Hamilton.
       A Short View of Elizabethan Drama.   New York:
       Scribner's, 1958.   pp. 69-74.   Passim.

388.   Ristine, F. H.   "Robert Greene," English Tragicom-
       edy.   New York: Columbia University Press,
       1910.   pp. 78-82.

389.   Roston, Murray.   Biblical Drama in England from
       the Middle Ages to the Present Day.   Evanston:
       Northwestern University Press, 1968.   Passim.

390. Schelling, F. E. The English Chronicle Play. New
      York: 1902. pp. 152-159, 166-168, passim.

391. Symonds, J. A. Shakespeare's Predecessors in the
      English Drama. London: Smith, Elder, 1900.
      pp. 537-563.

392. Talbert, Ernest W. Elizabethan Drama and Shake-
      speare's Early Plays. Chapel Hill: University
      of North Carolina Press, 1963. Passim.

393. Woodberry, G. E. "Greene's Place in Comedy," in
      Representative English Comedies by C. M. Gayley.
      I, passim.

394. ----. "Greene's Place in Comedy," in Studies of a
      Literateur. New York: Harcourt, Brace, 1921.
      pp. 241-251.

395. Wynne, Arnold. The Growth of English Drama. Ox-
      ford: Clarendon Press, 1914. pp. 146-167.

      (25) Robert Greene as a Poet

396. Adam, J. Q. "History of the Poem: What Thing Is
      Love?" MLN, 22 (November 1907), 225.

397. Arms, George and Locke, I. G. "Sweet Are the
      Thoughts," Explicator; 3 (February 1945), 27.

398. Briscoe, John P. (ed.). "Fair Samela," Tudor and
      Stuart Love Songs. London: Gay and Bird, 1902.
      pp. 39-40.

399. Brown, John Russell, and Harris, Bernard (eds.).
      Elizabethan Poetry (Stratford-Upon-Avon Studies
      2). London: Edward Arnold, 1960. pp. 44-47,
      49, 65.

400. Brydges, Sir Samuel E. "Criticism of Robert
      Greene's Poetry," Excerpta Tudoriana or Extracts
      from Elizabethan Literature, 2 volumes.

401. Bush, Douglas. Mythology and the Renaissance
      Tradition in English Poetry. New York: Norton,
      1932. Passim.

402.   Carpenter, F. I. "Tropes in Robert Greene," Meta-
        phor and Simile in the Minor Elizabethan Drama.
        Chicago: University of Chicago Press, 1895.
        pp. 55-62.

403.   Cibber, T. The Lives of the Poets of Great Britain
        and Ireland to the Times of Dean Swift. 5 vol-
        umes. London: R. Griffiths, 1753. Passim.

404.   Collier, John Payne. The History of English Drama-
        tic Poetry. London: 1831. Passim.

405.   ----. The Poetical Decameron. Edinburgh: Con-
        stable, 1820. Passim.

406.   Courthope, William John. A History of English
        Poetry. Volume II, New York: Macmillan, 1895-
        1910. Passim.

407.   Cowling, G. H. Music on the Shakespeare Stage.
        Cambridge: University Press, 1913. Passim.

408.   Cruttwell, Patrick. The Shakespearean Moment and
        Its Place in the Poetry of the Seventeenth Century.
        New York: Random House, 1960. pp. 34-58.

409.   Disraeli, Isaac. Calamities of Authors. New York:
        J. Eastburn, Eastburn, 1812. (* Illustrated by
        some account of a literary satire.).

410.   Drinkwater, J. English Poetry. London: Methuen,
        1938. pp. 131-133.

411.   Empson, William. Some Versions of the Pastoral.
        London: Chatto & Windus, 1935. pp. 31-34+.

412.   Erskine, John. The Elizabethan Lyric. New York:
        Columbia Press, 1903. pp. 116-119; 287-289+.

413.   Grundy, Joan. "Shakespeare's Sonnets and the
        Elizabethan Sonneteers," Shakespeare Survey, 15
        (1962), 41-49 [YWES, 43 (1962), 125].

414.   Harris, Lynn H. "Greene's Sephestia's Song to
        Her Child," Explicator, 5 (1946), Item 2.

415.   Hubbard, F. G.   "A Type of Blank Verse Found in
        the Earlier Elizabethan Drama," PMLA, 32
        (1917), 68-80.

416.   Ing, Catherine.   Elizabethan Lyrics.   New York:
        Barnes and Noble, 1951.   Passim.

417.   Langbaine, Gerard.   An Account of the English
        Dramatic Poets.   Oxford: G. West & H. Cle-
        ments, 1691.   pp. 241-243.

418.   Lavin, J. A.   "Two Notes on 'The Cobler's Prophecy':
        (1) The Court of Venus; (2) Greene's 'Sweet Are
        the Thoughts'," N & Q, 207 (April 1962), 137-
        139 [YWES, 43 (1962), 14].

419.   Lee, S.   "Robert Greene's Treatment of Venus and
        Adonis," in his edition of Shakespeare's Venus
        and Adonis.   Cambridge: (n. p.), 1905. pp. 30-
        31.

420.   Meynell, Alice C. T.   "Strictly an Elizabethan
        Lyricist," in her Second Person Singular and
        Other Essays.   London: Oxford University Press,
        1922. pp. 12-17.

421.   Minto, W.   Characteristics of English Poets from
        Chaucer to Shirley.   Boston: Ginn, 1889.   pp.
        311-319+.

422.   Moore, J. R.   "The Songs of the Public Theatres
        in the Time of Shakespeare," JEGP, 28 (April
        1929), 166-202.

423.   Pearson, Lu Emily.   Elizabethan Love Conventions.
        New York: Barnes and Noble, 1966[1933].

424.   Reardsibm, J. P. (ed.).   "A Maiden's Dream upon
        the Death of Christopher Batton; an Unknown
        Poetical Tract by Robert Greene," Shakespeare
        Society Papers, 2 (1845), 127-145.

425.   Reed, E. B.   English Lyrical Poetry.   New Haven:
        Yale University Press, 1912.   pp. 199-200.

426.   Rhys, E. Lyric Poetry. New York: J. M. Dent,
       1913. pp. 141-142.

427.   Schelling, Felix E. A Book of Elizabethan Lyrics.
       Boston: Ginn, 1895.

428.   Smart, G. K. "English Non-Dramatic Blank Verse
       in the Sixteenth Century," Anglia, 61 (1937), 392-
       393.

429.   Timberlake, Philip W. The Feminine Ending in
       English Blank Verse. Menasha, Wisconsin:
       Privately Printed, 1931. pp. 25-29.

430.   Tuve, Rosemond. Elizabethan and Metaphysical
       Imagery. Chicago: University of Chicago Press,
       1965[1947]. Passim.

(26) Robert Greene as Prose Writer

431.   Allen, Don C. "Science and Invention in Greene's
       Prose," PMLA, 53 (December 1938), 1117-1118.

432.   Ashley, Robert and Mosley, Edwin M. (eds.).
       Elizabethan Fiction. New York: Holt, Rinehart
       and Winston, 1965. pp. vii-xx.

433.   Atkins, J. W. H. "Elizabethan Prose Fiction," in
       CHEL, III, Chapter XVI, pp. 356-357.

434.   Austin, Warren B. "The Posthumous Greene Pam-
       phlets: A Computerized Study," SNL, 16 (Novem-
       ber-December 1966), 45.

435.   Baker, Ernest A. The History of the English Novel:
       the Elizabethan Age and After. London: H. F.
       and G. Whiterby, 1929. pp. 90-113.

436.   Beach, Donald Marcus. "Studies in the Art of
       Elizabethan Prose Narrative," Unpublished Ph. D.
       dissertation, Cornell University, 1959 [DA, 20
       (1959-60), Part 2, p. 2274].

437.   Bovinski, Ludwig. "The Origin of the Euphuistic
       Novel and Its Significance of Shakespeare," in
       Studies in Honor of T. W. Baldwin. Urbana:
       University of Illinois Press, 1958. pp. 38-52.

438.   Carroll, William Meredith. Animal Conventions in
        English Renaissance Non-Religious Prose (1550-
        1600). New York: Bookman Associates, 1954.
        Passim.

439.   Dunlop, J. The History of Fiction. Edinburgh:
        Longman, Hurst, Rees, Orne, and Brown, 1816.
        III, 436-446.

440.   Goree, Roselle Gould. "Concerning Repetitions in
        Greene's Romances," PQ, 3 (1924), 69-75.

441.   Grosart, Alexander B. (ed.). The Life and Complete
        Works in Prose and Verse of Robert Greene,
        M. A. Volume I: Strojenko's Life of Robert
        Greene with Introduction and Notes. pp. 65-116.

442.   Hart, H. C. "Greene's Prose Works," N & Q, 112
        (July 1, 1905), 1-5; 81-84; (July 29), 162-164;
        (August 26), 224-227; (September 16), 484-485;
        (December 16), 113; (February 3, 1906), 84-85;
        202-204.

443.   ----. "Greene's Prose Works," N & Q, 112 (July
        1, 1905), 1-5.

444.   Herford, C. H. "A Few Suggestions on Greene's
        Romances and Shakespeare," Transactions of the
        New Shakespeare Society (1887-1892), II, 181-
        190.

445.   Hornat, Jaroslav. "Mamilla: Robert Greene's Con-
        troversy with Euphues," Philologica Pragensia, 5
        (1962), 210-218.

446.   Hurrell, J. D. "Themes and Conventions of Eliza-
        bethan Prose Fiction (1588-1603)," Unpublished
        Ph. D. dissertation. University of Birmingham,
        1954-55. (Index, V, 8).

447.   Judges, A. V. (ed.). The Elizabethan Underworld.
        New York: Dutton, 1930. pp. 119-178; 498-502.
        Passim.

448.   Jusserand, Jean J. English Novel in the Time of
        Shakespeare. New York: Barnes and Nobles,
        1967 [c. 1901]. Passim.

449.   Krapp, G. P.   The Rise of English Literary Prose.
        New York: Oxford University Press, 1915.   pp.
        492-502.

450.   Lavin, J. A.   "The Cobler's Prophecy," N & Q,
        207 (April 1962), 137-139.   [YWES, 43 (1962),
        14].

451.   Lawlor, John.   "Pandosto and the Nature of Dramatic
        Romance," PQ, 41(1962), 96-113.

452.   Marder, Louis.   "Greene's Attack on Shakespeare:
        A Posthumous Hoax?" SNL, 16 (September 1966),
        29-30.

453.   Routh, Harold V.   "London and the Development of
        Popular Literature," CHEL, IV, Chapter XVI,
        318-319.

454.   Schelling, Felix E.   "Pamphlet and the Prose of
        Controversy," English Literature during the Life-
        time of Shakespeare. London: George Bell, 1910.

455.   Schlauch, Margaret.   Antecedents of the English
        Novel, 1400-1600.   New York: Oxford University
        Press, 1963 [YWES, 44 (1963), 191].

456.   Staton, Walter F. , Jr.   "The Characters of Style in
        Elizabethan Prose," Journal of English and
        Germanic Philology, 57 (April 1958), 197-207
        [YWES, 39 (1958), 102-103, and 164].

457.   Sutherland, James.   On English Prose (The Alexander
        Lectures, 1950-57).   Toronto University Press,
        1957.   passim.   [YWES, 39 (1958), 27].

458.   Tuckerman, B.   A History of English Prose Fiction.
        New York: Putnam's, 1882.   pp. 83-88.

459.   Utterback, E. I.   "Characteristics of the Novel as
        Exemplified in Robert Greene's Pamphlets," Uni-
        versity of Oklahoma Bulletin, January 1939.   pp.
        118-119.

460.   Vincent, L. H.   "An Elizabethan Novelist," The Bib-
        liotaph, and Other People.   Boston: Houghton,

Mifflin, 1899. pp. 137-164.
(Reprint from Poet Lore.)

461.   Weld, J. S.   "Some Problems of Euphuistic Narra-
       tive: Robert Greene and Henry Wotton," SP, 45
       (April 1948), 165-171.

462.   Winny, James (ed.).   The Descent of Euphues.
       Columbia University Press, 1957.   Reviewed by
       G. K. Hunter in RES, 10 (1959), 329; by L. G.
       Salingar in DUJ, 20 (1959), 85-86; by I. Simon
       in RLV, (1959), 51-52 [YWES, 38 (1957), 167].

463.   Winstanley, William.   Lives of the Most Famous
       English Poets (1687).   A Facsimile Production.
       Gainesville, Florida: Scholar's Facsimiles &
       Reprints, 1963.

464.   Wolff, S. L.   The Greek Romances in Elizabethan
       Prose Fiction.   New York: Columbia University
       Press, 1912.   pp. 376-456.

B.   Criticism (Articles and Discussions in Books)

465.   Acheson, Arthur. Shakespeare, Chapman and Sir
         Thomas More. New York: Edmond Byrne Hackett,
         1931.

466.   Adams, J. Q. "Menaphon and The Thracian Wonder,"
         MP, 3 (January 1906), 317-326.

467.   Albright, Evelyn May. Dramatic Publication in
         England, 1580-1640: A Study of Conditions Affect-
         ing Content and Form of Drama. Boston: D. C.
         Heath, 1927; London: Oxford University Press,
         1927. Passim.

468.   Allen, Don C. "Science and Invention in Robert
         Greene's Prose," PMLA, 53 (December 1938),
         1007-1018.

469.   Baker, G. P. (ed.). CHEL. 15 volumes. Cam-
         bridge: University Press, 1910. Passim.

470.   Baker, Hershel. The Image of Man. New York:
         Harper, 1961. "The Renaissance View of Man."

471.   Baldwin, Charles Sears. Renaissance Literary
         Theory and Practice: Classicism in the Rhetoric
         and Poetic of Italy, France, and England 1400-1600.
         Gloucester, Mass.: Peter Smith, 1959[c. 1939],
         p. 201.

472.   Baldwin, Thomas W. On the Literary Genetics of
         Shakespeare's Plays 1592-1594. Urbana: Uni-
         versity of Illinois, 1959. pp. 1-55, 56-104. 514-
         520, 524-534.

473.   Baskerville, Charles R. et al (eds.). Elizabethan
         and Stuart Plays. New York: Holt, Rinehart
         and Winston, 1934. Passim.

474.   Baxter, J. P. The Greatest of Literary Problems.
         Boston: Houghton, Mifflin, 1915. pp. 479-480.

475.   Bayley, H.   The Shakespeare Symphony.   London:
       Chapman & Hall, 1906.   Passim.

476.   Bennett, Josephine W. , et al (eds.).   Studies in the
       English Renaissance Drama.   New York: Uni-
       versity Press, 1959.   Passim.

477.   Berereton, J. Le G.   Elizabethan Drama.   Sydney:
       (n. p.), 1909.   pp. 16-36.

478.   ----.   Writings on Elizabethan Drama.   Victoria,
       Australia: Melbourne University Press, 1948.

479.   Boas, Frederick S.   An Introduction to Tudor Drama.
       London: Oxford University Press, 1946 [c. 1933].

480.   ----.   Shakespeare and His Predecessors.   London:
       Murray, 1896.

481.   Bottrall, Margaret (comp.).   Personal Records.
       London: R. Hart-Davis, 1961.   pp. 79-81, 223.

482.   Bovinski, Ludwig.   "The Origin of the Euphuistic
       Novel and Its Significance of Shakespeare," in
       Studies in Honor of T. W. Baldwin.   Urbana:
       University of Illinois Press, 1958.   pp.   38-52.

483.   Bowers, Fredson.   Elizabethan Revenge Tragedy
       1587-1642.   Gloucester, Mass. :   Peter Smith,
       1940.

484.   Bradbrook, Muriel C.   English Dramatic Form: A
       History of Its Development.   New York: Barnes
       and Noble, 1965.

485.   ----.   The Growth and Structure of Elizabethan
       Comedy.   Baltimore: Penguin Books, 1963
       [c. 1955].

486.   ----.   The Rise of the Common Player; A Study of
       Actor and Society in Shakespeare's England.   Har-
       vard University Press, 1962.

487.   ----.   Themes and Conventions of Elizabethan
       Tragedy.   Cambridge: University Press, 1957.

488.   Bradley, Henry.   "Some Textual Puzzles in Greene's
       Works," MLR, 1 (April 1906), 208-211.

489.   Bradley, J. F. and Adams, J. Q. (ed.).   "Allusion
       to Robert Greene," in their The Jonson Allusion
       Book, 1597-1700.   New Haven: Yale University
       Press, 1922.   Passim.

490.   Brooke, C. F. Tucker.   The Renaissance (1500-1660).
       (Volume II of A Literary History of England ed.
       by Albert C. Baugh).   New York: Appleton-
       Century-Crofts, 1948.

491.   ----.   The Tudor Drama: A History of English
       National Drama to the Retirement of Shakespeare.
       Hamden, Conn.:   Archon Books, 1964. [c. 1911].
       pp. 263-270, passim.

492.   Browne, C. E.   "Greene's Allusion to the Stage,"
       N & Q, 51 (March 20, 1775), 224-225.

493.   Bubb, Laurence.   The Elizabethan Malady: A Study
       of Melancholia in English Literature from 1580
       to 1640.   East Lansing: Michigan State College
       Press, 1951 [Planetomachia, pp. 88-89, A Look-
       ing Glasse, p. 119+.   Passim].

494.   Bush, Douglas.   Mythology and the Renaissance
       Tradition in English Poetry.   Minneapolis: Uni-
       versity of Minnesota Press, 1932.   Passim.

495.   Camp, C. W.   The Artisan in Elizabethan Literature.
       New York: Columbia University Press, 1932.
       pp. 86-91.

496.   Cartwright, Robert.   The Footsteps of Shakespeare;
       or A Ramble with the Early Dramatists.   London:
       John Russell Smith, 1892.

497.   Carroll, William M.   Animal Conventions in English
       Renaissance Non-Religious Prose (1550-1600).
       New York: Bookman Associates, 1954.   passim.

498.   Castle, E. J.   Shakespeare, Bacon, Jonson, and
       Greene.   London: S. , Low, Marston, 1897.   pp.
       155-166.

499.   Cawley, R. R.   The Voyagers and Elizabethan Drama.
        Boston: Heath, 1938. Passim.

500.   Chambers, E. K.   "Allusions to Greene and His
        Works," The Shakespeare Allusion-Book, ed. by
        C. M. Ingleby et al. London: Oxford University
        Press, 1932. Passim.

501.   ----. The Elizabethan Stage. 4 volumes. Oxford:
        Clarendon Press, 1923.

502.   Chandler, F. W.   The Literature of Roguery. Boston:
        Houghton Mifflin, 1907.

503.   Clarkson, Paul S. and Warren, Clyde T.   The Law
        of Property in Shakespeare and the Elizabethan
        Drama. Baltimore: Johns Hopkins Press, 1942.
        Passim.

504.   Collier, John Payne.   The History of English Dra-
        matic Poetry to the Time of Shakespeare: and
        Annals of The Stage to the Restoration. 3 vol-
        umes. London: Bell, 1879 [c. 1831], passim.

505.   ----. "Robert Greene in the Stationers' Register,"
        N & Q, 23-24 (July 6, 1861 to November 29,
        1862), passim.

506.   Collins, John Churton.   Essays and Studies. London:
        Macmillan, 1895.

507.   ----. (ed.). The Plays and Poems of Robert
        Greene. 2 volumes. Oxford: Clarendon Press,
        1905, II, General Introduction.

508.   Craig, Hardin.   The Literature of the English Ren-
        aissance 1485-1660. Volume II of A History of
        English Literature, ed. by Hardin Craig. New
        York: Collier Books, 1962.

509.   Crane, T. F.   Italian Social Customs of the Six-
        teenth Century. New Haven: Yale University
        Press, 1920.

510.   Creizenach, W.   The English Drama in the Age of
        Shakespeare. Philadelphia: Lippincott, 1916.

511. Curry, John V. Deception in Elizabethan Comedy.
      Chicago: Loyola University Press, 1955.

512. Day, Martin S. History of English Literature to
      1660. Garden City, New York: Doubleday, 1963.
      Passim.

513. Dean, James S. , Jr. "Antedatings from Robert
      Greene," N & Q, 208 (August 1963), 296-298.

514. Dickinson, Thomas H. (ed.). Robert Greene.
      London: T. Fisher Unwin, (n. d.).
      (The Mermaid Series.)

515. Downer, Alan S. The British Drama. New York:
      Appleton-Century-Crofts, 1950.

516. Dyce, Alexander (ed.). The Dramatic Works of
      Robert Greene. London: William Pickering, 1831.

517. Empson, William. "The Function of the Double Plot,"
      in Shakespeare's Contemporaries, ed. by Max
      Bluestone and Norman Rabkin. Englewood Cliffs,
      New Jersey: Prentice-Hall, 1961. pp. 34ff.
      [Originally in his Some Versions of Pastoral.
      London: Chatto and Windus, 1935. pp. 27-34.]

518. Esler, Anthony. "Robert Greene and the Spanish
      Armada," ELH, 32 (September 1965), 314-332.

519. Evans, Sir Ifor. A Short History of English Drama.
      Boston: Houghton Mifflin, 1965. pp. 38, 43-44,
      47.
      (* Riverside Studies in Literature.)

520. Fansler, Harriott Ely. The Evolution of Technic in
      Elizabethan Tragedy. Chicago and New York:
      Row, Peterson and Company, 1914.

521. Farnham, Willard. The Medieval Heritage of Eliz-
      abethan Tragedy. Berkeley: University of Cali-
      fornia Press, 1936.

522. Fleay, Frederick Gard. A Biographical Chronicle of
      the English Drama, 1559-1642. London: Reeves
      and Turner, 1891.

523.   ----.   A Chronicle History of the Life and Works of
        William Shakespeare, Player, Poet and Playmaker.
        London: J. C. Nimmo, 1886.

524.   Fluchere, Henri.   Shakespeare and the Elizabethans.
        Tr. by Guy Hamilton.   New York: Hill and Wang,
        1961.   Passim.
        (Introduced by T. S. Eliot.)

525.   Ford, Boris (ed.).   The Age of Shakespeare.   Bal-
        timore: Penguin Books, 1962.   pp. 57-59; 124-
        125.

526.   Freeburg, Victor Oscar.   Disguise Plots in Eliza-
        bethan Drama: A Study in Stage Tradition.   New
        York: Columbia University Press, 1915.   pp.
        199-205.

527.   Freeman, Arthur.   "Two Notes on A Knack to Con-
        troversy with Euphues," Philologia Pragensia, 5
        (1962), 210-218; N & Q, 207 (September 1962),
        326-327.

528.   ----.   "An Unacknowledged Work of Robert Greene,"
        N & Q, 210 (October 1965), 378-379.

529.   Gayley, Charles Mills.   Representative English Com-
        edies From the Beginnings to Shakespeare.   2
        volumes.   New York: Macmillan, 1930.

530.   Gibson, J. P. S. R.   "The Supernatural in Shakes-
        peare's Contemporaries," Shakespeare's Use of
        the Supernatural.   Cambridge: Deighton, Bell,
        1908.   pp. 86-110.

531.   Gosse, Edmund W.   Seventeenth Century Studies.
        London: William Heinemann, 1914.

532.   Greg, W. W. (ed.).   A Looking-glass for London and
        England By Thomas Lodge and Robert Greene,
        1594.   London: Malone Society, 1932.   "Intro-
        duction. "

533.   ----.   "A Review of J. C. Collins's The Plays and
        Poems of Robert Greene," MLR, 1 (April 1906),
        238-251.

534.   Hall, Vernon, Jr. Renaissance Literary Criticism:
        A Study of Its Social Content. Gloucester, Mass. :
        Peter Smith, 1959 [c. 1945]. p. 218.

535.   Harrison, George B. (ed.). The Elizabethan Journals.
        2 volumes. Garden City, New York: Doubleday,
        1965. Passim.

536.   Harvey, Sir Paul (ed.). The Oxford Companion to
        English Literature. Oxford: Clarendon Press,
        1955.

537.   Hatcher, O. L. "The Sources and Authorship of the
        Thracian Wonder," MLN, 23 (January 1908), 16-
        20.

538.   Hayashi, Tetsumaro. "An Edition of A Looking
        Glasse for London and England By Thomas Lodge
        and Robert Greene," Unpublished Ph. D. disserta-
        tion, Kent State University, 1968. pp. 1-62.

539.   Holmes, Elizabeth. Aspects of Elizabethan Imagery.
        Oxford: Basil Blackwell, 1929.

540.   Honigmann, E. A. J. "Shakespeare's Lost Source-
        Plays," MLR, 49 (July 1954), 293-297.

541.   Hosley, Richard (ed.). Essays on Shakespeare and
        Elizabethan in Honor of Hardin Craig. Columbia:
        University of Missouri Press, 1962. pp. 45-54,
        passim.

542.   Hubbard, F. G. "Repetition and Parallelism in the
        Earlier Elizabethan Drama," PMLA, 20 (1905),
        360-379.

543.   Ing, Catherine. Elizabethan Lyrics. New York:
        Barnes and Noble, 1951. Passim.

544.   Jewkes, Wilfred T. Act Division in Elizabethan and
        Jacobean Plays 1583-1616. New York: Shoe
        String Press, 1958.

545.   Joseph, Sister Miriam. Rhetoric in Shakespeare's
        Time. New York: Harcourt, Brace, and World,
        1962. Passim. [part of the work Shakespeare's
        Use of the Arts of Language, Columbia Univer-

sity Press, c. 1947].

546.   Judges, A. V. (ed.). The Elizabethan Underworld.
       New York: Dutton, 1930.

547.   Klein, David. The Elizabethan Dramatists as Critics.
       New York: Philosophical Library, 1963. Passim.

548.   Lavin, J. A. "Two Notes on The Cobler's Prophecy, "
       N & Q, 207 (April 1962), 137-139.
       (* 1. "The Court of Venus," and 2. "Greene's
       'Sweet Are the Thought.' ")

549.   Lee, Sidney. The French Renaissance in England.
       New York: Oxford University Press, 1910.

550.   Lewis, C. S. English Literature in the Sixteenth
       Century Excluding Drama. Oxford: Clarendon
       Press, 1965.

551.   Lievsay, John L. "Greene's Panther: A Mixture
       of Tradition and Invention," P. Q. , 20 (1941), 296-
       303.

552.   ----. Stefano Guazzo and the English Renaissance,
       1575-1675. Chapel Hill, N. C. : University of
       North Carolina Press, 1961. pp. 99-107.

553.   McKerrow, R. B. "J. C. Jordan's Robert Greene, "
       MLR, 11 (April 1916), 233-235.

554.   McNeal, Thomas H. "The Literary Origins of Robert
       Greene," Shakespeare Association Bulletin, 14
       (1939), 176-181.

555.   McNeir, Waldo F. "Greene's Medievalization of
       Ariosto," RLC, 29 (1955), 351-360.

556.   Manly, John Matthews. Specimens of the Pre-
       Shakespearean Drama. Boston: Ginn, 1897. Vol.
       II [James IV, pp. 329-418, annotated and collated].

557.   "Martine Mar-Sextus (1592) and Robert Greene, "
       N & Q, 110 (December 17, 1904), 483-484.

558. Maxwell, B. "Original of Sir John Falstaff: Believe
      It or Not," SP, 27 (April 30), 230-232.

559. Maxwell, J. C. "Greene's Ridstall Man," MLR, 44
      (January 1949), 88.

560. Miller, Edwin H. "The Pamphlets of Robert Greene,
      1591-1592," Unpublished Ph. D. dissertation, Har-
      vard University, 1955. DD, 18 (1950-51), 226.

561. Miller, E. Madge. "Greene, Robert," Encyclopaedia
      Britannica, 10 (1963), 855-856.

562. Mills, L. J. "Robert Greene," in One Soul in Bodies
      Twain. Bloomington, Indiana: Indiana University
      Press, 1937. pp. 196-214, 250-253.

563. Mithal, H. S. D. "The Authorship of Fair Em and
      Martin Mar-Sixtus," N & Q, 205 (January 1960),
      8-10 [Mourning Garment].

564. Morley, H. English Writers. London: Chapman
      & Hall, 1892. IX, 212-226; 268-279.

565. Morris, Helen. Elizabethan Literature. London:
      Oxford University Press, 1958. Passim.

566. Moulton, C. W. The Library of Literary Criticism.
      Buffalo: Moulton, 1901. pp. 339-345.

567. Muir, Kenneth. "Robert Greene as Dramatist," in
      Essays on Shakespeare and Elizabethan Drama in
      Honor of Hardin Craig. Passim.

568. Neilson, William Allan (ed.). The Chief Elizabethan
      Dramatists Excluding Shakespeare, Selected Plays.
      Boston: Houghton Mifflin, 1911.

569. O'Conner, J. J. "On the Authorship of the Ratsey
      Pamphlets," PQ, 30 (October 1951), 381-386.

570. Otis, William Bradley, and Needleman, Morris H.
      An Outline-History of English Literature. New
      York: Barnes and Noble, 1952. I, 153-154.

571. Paradise, N. Burton. Thomas Lodge: The History
      of an Elizabethan. New Haven: Yale University

          Press, 1931.

572.   Parrott, Thomas Marc and Ball, Robert Hamilton.
       A Short View of Elizabethan Drama.   New York:
       Scribner's, 1958[c. 1943].

573.   "Plays and Poems. A Review," Nation, 82 (May
       17, 1906), 410-411.

574.   "Plays of the University Wits," CHEL, V, 148-155.

575.   "The Predecessors of Shakespeare," Quarterly Re-
       view, 161 (October 1885), 367-374.

576.   Quaintance, Richard E., Jr. "The French Source
       of Robert Greene's What Thing Is Love," N & Q,
       208 (August 1963), 295-296.

577.   Rae, Wesley D. Thomas Lodge. New York:
       Twayne, 1967.

578.   Reed, Robert R., Jr. The Occult in the Tudor and
       Stuart Stage.   Boston: Christopher Publishing
       House, 1965. [Friar Bacon, pp. 101-106, passim].

579.   Renwick, W. L. "Greene's Ridstall Man," MLR, 29
       (October 1934), 434.

580.   Ribner, Irving. The English History Play in the Age
       of Shakespeare.   Princeton University Press,
       1957.

581.   ----. Jacobean Tragedy: The Quest for Moral
       Order. New York: Barnes and Noble, 1962.

582.   "Robert Greene," Bibliotheca Heberiana (London),
       (1834-1836), 113-115.

583.   "Robert Greene," Edinburgh Review, 71 (July 1840),
       470 ff.

584.   Robertson, John M. Did Shakespeare Write Titus
       Andronicus? London: Watts, 1905 [Many refer-
       ences in the Index plus Chapter II Greene's Un-
       signed Works, pp. 141-175].

585. Rossiter, A. P. English Drama from Early Time to
      the Elizabethans: Its Background, Origins and
      Developments. New York: Barnes and Noble,
      1959.

586. Routh, Harold V. "London and the Development of
      Popular Literature," CHEL, Chapter XVI, 316-
      321.

587. Sanders, Norman. "The Comedy of Greene and
      Shakespeare," in Early Shakespeare (Stratford-
      Upon-Avon Studies, 3). London: Edward Arnold,
      1961. pp. 35-54.

588. ----. "Greene's Tamiluolin," N & Q, 207 (June
      1962), 229-230.

589. Schelling, Felix E. Elizabethan Drama 1559-1642.
      2 volumes. Boston: Houghton, Mifflin, 1908;
      New York: Russell & Russell, 1958.

590. ----. The Queen's Progress. Boston: Houghton,
      Mifflin, 1904. pp. 131-147.

591. ----; and Black, Matthew. (eds.). Typical Eliza-
      bethan Plays by Contemporaries and Immediate
      Successors of Shakespeare. New York: Harper,
      1931.

592. Scott, T. J. "Early Rarity of the Works of Robert
      Greene," The Papers of the Shakespeare Society.
      London: Shakespeare Society, 1853. I, 83-87.

593. Secombe, Thomas and Allen, J. W. The Age of
      Shakespeare. London: Bell, 1911. 2 vols.
      Passim.

594. Sheavyn, Phoebe. The Literary Profession in the
      Elizabethan Age. New York: Haskell House,
      1964 [c. 1906].

595. Simpson, Percy. Studies in Elizabethan Drama.
      Oxford: Clarendon Press, 1955.

596. Simpson, Richard (ed.). The School of Shakespeare.
      2 volumes. London: Chatto & Windus, 1878.

597.   ----. "On Some Plays Attributed to Shakespeare,"
        Transactions of the New Shakespeare Society,
        1875-76. London: N. S. S. , 1904. I, 155-180.

598.   Sisson, Charles J. (ed.). Thomas Lodge and Other
        Elizabethans. Cambridge: Harvard University
        Press, 1933.

599.   Smith, G. Gregory, (ed). Elizabethan Critical Essays.
        Oxford: Clarendon Press, 1904.

600.   Spencer, Hazelton (ed.). Elizabethan Plays. Boston:
        Heath, 1933. [His introductory essays, passim.]

601.   Spencer, Theodore. Death and Elizabethan Tragedy:
        A Study of Convention and Opinion in the Eliza-
        bethan Drama. Cambridge: Harvard University
        Press, 1936.

602.   Tenney, Edward Andrew. Thomas Lodge. Ithaca:
        Cornell University Press, 1935.

603.   T. H. K. "Robert Greene," Dramatic Monthly, 2
        (April 1830), 70-75.

604.   Thorndike, Ashley H. English Comedy. New York:
        Macmillan, 1929. pp. 89-93.

605.   Tillyard, E. M. W. Shakespeare's History Plays.
        New York: Collier Books, 1962 [c. 1944].

606.   Tuve, Rosemond. Elizabethan and Metaphysical
        Imagery: Renaissance Poetic and Twentieth Century
        Critics. Chicago: University of Chicago Press,
        1965 [c. 1947].

607.   Vincent, Charles J. "Further Repetitions in the
        Works of Robert Greene," PQ, 18 (1939), 73-77.

608.   Wann, L. "The Oriental in Elizabethan Drama,"
        MP, 12 (January 1915), 423-427.

609.   Ward, A. W. A History of English Dramatic Litera-
        ture to the Death of Queene Anne. London: Ox-
        ford University Press, 1875.

(Marlowe's <u>Faustus</u> and Greene's <u>Friar Bacon</u>.
<u>Passim.</u>)

610.   Wells, Henry W.   <u>Elizabethan and Jacobean Play-</u>
        <u>wrights.</u> New York: Columbia University Press,
        1939.

611.   Wells, Stanley W.   "Impartial," <u>N & Q</u>, 207 (Octo-
        ber 1959), 353-354.

        [*Greene's <u>Perymedes the Black Smith</u> (1588).]

612.   ----.   "Some Words in 1588," <u>N & Q</u>, 207 (June
        1962), 205-207.

613.   Wilson, Frank Percy.   <u>Elizabethan and Jacobean.</u>
        Oxford: Clarendon Press, 1945.

614.   Winny, James (ed.).   <u>The Descent of Euphues.</u>
        <u>Three Elizabethan Romance Stories: Euphues,</u>
        <u>Pandosto, Piers Plainness.</u> Cambridge: Univer-
        sity Press, 1957.

615.   Woodward, Parker.   <u>Euphues the Peripatician.</u>
        (Attributing to Francis Bacon the Authorship of
        the Works of Robert Greene). London: Gay and
        Bird, 1907.

616.   Wright, H. G.   "The Ridstall Man, in <u>James IV</u>,"
        <u>MLR,</u> 30 (July 1935), p. 347.

617.   Wright, Louis B.   <u>Middle Class Culture in Eliza-</u>
        <u>bethan England.</u> University of North Carolina
        Press, 1935. <u>Passim.</u>

618.   ----.   <u>Shakespeare for Everyman.</u> New York:
        Washington Square Press, 1964. <u>Passim.</u>

C.   Biography

619.   Allen, Ned B.   "Shakespeare's Achievement," <u>SNL</u>,
        12 (April 1962), 16 [a review of Ward T. Price's
        essay, "Shakespeare and His Young Contempor-
        aries," <u>PQ</u>, 41 (January 1962), 37-57.]

620.   Aydelotte, Frank.   <u>Elizabethan Rogues and Vagabonds</u>
        <u>in Oxford Historical and Literary Studies.</u>   Ox-
        ford: Clarendon Press, 1913.   I, <u>passim</u>.

621.   Baker, D. E. <u>et al</u> (eds.).   "Robert Greene," <u>Bio-</u>
        <u>graphia Dramatica</u> (London), I (1812), 296-298.

622.   Baker, G. P.   <u>CHEL</u>, V, pp. 121-141, <u>passim</u>.

623.   Bentley, Gerald Eades.   <u>Shakespeare: A Biographical</u>
        <u>Handbook</u>.   New Haven: Yale University Press,
        1962.   pp.   94-97.

624.   Berkenhout, John.   <u>Biographia Literaria</u>.   London:
        Dodsley, 1777.   pp. 389-392.

625.   Boas, F. S.   <u>Shakespeare and His Predecessors</u>.
        New York: Scribner's, 1902.   pp.   77-88.

626.   Brooke, C. F. Tucker.   <u>The Renaissance (1500-1600)</u>
        (Volume II of <u>A Literary History of England</u> ed.
        Albert C. Baugh.   New York: Appleton-Century-
        Crofts, 1948.

627.   Bullen, A. H.   "Robert Greene," in <u>DNB</u>.   III, 509-
        511.

628.   Cawley, Robert Ralston.   <u>The Voyagers and Eliza-</u>
        <u>bethan Drama.</u>   Boston: Heath, 1938.

629.   Chettle, Henry.   <u>Kindheart's Dreame</u>, ed. G. B.
        Harrison.   London: C. Richard, 1923.

630.   Cooper, Charles Henry and Cooper, Thomas.
        <u>Athenae Cantabrigienses</u>.   2 volumes.   Cambridge:
        Deighton Bell, 1858-1913.   II, 127-135.

631. Day, Martin S. History of English Literature to
      1660. Garden City, New York: Doubleday, 1963.
      I, Passim.

632. Dewar, R. "Robert Greene," Reading University
      College Review, 6 (1914), 115-138.

633. Drew, Philip. "Was Greene's Young Juvenal Nashe
      or Lodge?" Studies in English Literature, 1500-
      1900. 7 (Winter 1967), 55-66.

634. Dunham, S. A. Lives of the Most Eminent Literary
      and Scientific Men of Great Britain. London:
      Brown, Green and Logmans, 1840. pp. 22-49.

635. Erskine, John. "Greene, Robert," Encyclopedia
      Americana, 13 (1967), 430-431.

636. "Greene, Robert (1558-1592)," in The Reader's
      Encyclopedia of Shakespeare. ed. Oscar J. Camp-
      bell and Edward G. Quinn. New York: Crowell,
      1966. pp. 271-272.

637. Gayley, Charles Mills. Representative English Com-
      edies. I, 397-402.

638. Gosse, Edmund W. (ed.). "Memoir of Thomas
      Lodge," in The Complete Works of Thomas Lodge.
      New York: Russell and Russell, 1963 [c. 1883].
      I, 1-46.

639. "Greene, Robert (1560?-1592)," Oxford Companion
      to English Literature ed. Sir Paul Harvey. Ox-
      ford: Clarendon Press, 1955. p. 337.

640. Greg, W. W. (ed.). Henslowe's Diary. 3 volumes.
      London: A. H. Bullen, 1904-1908.

641. Grosart, Alexander B. (ed.). See Strojenko.

642. Halliday, F. E. "Greene, Robert (1558-1592)," in
      his A Shakespeare Companion 1550-1950. London:
      Gerald Duckworth, 1952. pp. 246-247.

643. Harrison, G. B. Elizabethan Plays and Players. Ann
      Arbor: University of Michigan Press, 1961.

644.   Henslowe's Diary.   See Greg, W. W. (ed.).

645.   "The Homer of Women," Academy, 69 (December 2,
       1905), 1252-1253.

646.   Hodgetts, E. A. B. (tr.).   See Strojenko.

647.   Kunitz, Stanley J. and Haycraft, Howard (eds.).
       "Greene, Robert (July 1558-September 3, 1592),"
       in British Authors Before 1800. New York: H. W.
       Wilson, 1961. pp. 235-236.

648.   Lewis, C. S. English Literature in the Sixteenth
       Century Excluding Drama.   Oxford: Clarendon
       Press, 1965. Passim.

649.   Livesay, John L. "Robert Greene, Master of Arts,
       and Mayster Guazzo," SP, 36 (October 1939),
       577-596.

650.   Mildenberger, K. "Robert Greene at Cambridge,"
       MLN, 66 (December 1951), 546-549.

651.   Miller, E. Madge. "Greene, Robert," Encyclopaedia
       Britannica, 10 (1963), 855-856.

652.   Paradise, N. Burton. Thomas Lodge: The History
       of An Elizabethan. New Haven: Yale University
       Press, 1931. Passim.

653.   Parr, Johnstone. "Robert Greene and His Class-
       mates at Cambridge," PMLA, 77 (December 1962),
       536-543.

654.   Parrott, Thomas M. and Ball, Robert H. A Short
       View of Elizabethan Drama. New York:
       Scribner's, 1958.

655.   Price, Ward T. "Shakespeare and His Young Con-
       temporaries," PQ, 41 (January 1962), 37-57.

656.   Rae, Wesley D. Thomas Lodge. New York:
       Twayne, 1967. Passim.

657.   "Robert Greene," TLS, August 17, 1916. p. 390.

658.   Schelling, Felix E.   "Typical Elizabethan," Saturday
        Review of Literature, 9 (July 30, 1932), 18.

659.   Sisson, Charles J. (ed.).   Thomas Lodge and Other
        Elizabethans.   Cambridge: Harvard University
        Press, 1933.

660.   Strojenko, Nicholas.   "Robert Greene: His Life and
        Works, A Critical Investigation," Moscow, 1878),
        tr. from the Russian by E. A. Brayley Hodgetts,
        in The Life and Complete Works in Prose and
        Verse of Robert Greene, M. A. , ed. A. R. Grosart.
        pp. 1-256.

661.   Thorndike, Ashley H.   English Comedy.   New York:
        Macmillan, 1929.

662.   Venn, J. and N. A.   Alumni Cantabrigiensis.   Cam-
        bridge: University Press, 1922.

663.   Walker, Roy J.   "Robert Greene, 1560-1592, Drama-
        tist," Hobbies, 63 (May 1958), 107+.

664.   Wood, Anthony.   Athenae Oxonienses.   London: R.
        Knaplock and D. Widwinter, and J. Ronson, 1721.

D.   Books, Monographs, and Pamphlets

665.   Berereton, John Le Gay. Tomorrow: A Dramatic
         Sketch of the Character and Environment of Robert
         Greene. Sydney: 1910.

666.   Hayashi, Tetsumaro. A Textual Study of A Looking
         Glasse for London and England by Thomas Lodge
         and Robert Greene. Muncie, Indiana: Ball State
         University, 1969 [BSU Monograph Series].

667.   Herford, C. H. Greene's Romances and Shakespeare.
         Transactions of the New Shakespeare Society.
         1888. Passim.

668.   Hodgetts, E. A. B. (tr.). See Strojenko, Nicholas.

669.   Jordan, J. C. Robert Greene. New York: Columbia
         University Press, 1915; New York: Octagon Books,
         1965.

670.   Parr, Johnstone, and Shapiro, I. A. Instructions to
         Editors of the Works of Robert Greene. Birming-
         ham, England: Shakespeare Institute, University
         of Birmingham, 1959.

671.   ----, et al. List of Edition, Copies, and Locations
         of the Works of Robert Greene. Shakespeare
         Institute, 1958.

672.   Saunders, Chauncey. Robert Greene and the Harveys.*
         Indiana University Studies (no. 93). Bloomington,
         Indiana, 1931.

         (*Richard, John, and Gabriel Harvey.)

673.   Strojenko, Nicholas. Robert Greene: His Life and
         Works. tr. by E. A. B. Hodgetts. Volume I of
         the Grosart Edition.

E.   Unpublished Dissertations and Theses

674.   Beach, Donald Marcus. "Studies in the Art of
        Elizabethan Prose Narrative," Unpublished Ph. D.
        dissertation.   Cornell University, 1959 [DA, 20
        (1959-60), Pt. 1, p. 2274].

675.   Clugston, George Alan. "A Looking Glass for Lon-
        don and England, By Thomas Lodge and Robert
        Greene. A Critical Edition," Unpublished Ph. D.
        Dissertation, University of Michigan, 1967.

676.   Cotham, Margaret Mary. "Greene and Lodge's A
        Looking-glass for London and England," Unpub-
        lished M. A. Thesis, University of Texas, 1928.

677.   Doherty, Paul Colman. "The Prose Works of Robert
        Greene," Unpublished Ph. D. Dissertation, Univ-
        ersity of Missouri, 1964.   [D. A. , 35 (1964), 5926-
        5927.]

678.   Hayashi, Tetsumaro. "An Edition of A Looking
        Glasse for London and England by Thomas Lodge
        and Robert Greene," Unpublished Ph. D. Disser-
        tation, Kent State University, 1968.

679.   Kendall, Jack L.   "The Relation Between the Plays
        and the Romances of Robert Greene," Unpublished
        Ph. D. Dissertation, Yale University, 1955.

680.   Kocher, P. H.   "The Ethics of the Early Elizabethan
        Drama as Exemplified in the Plays of Lyly, Mar-
        lowe, Greene, Peele, Lodge, and Nashe," Stan-
        ford University Bulletin, 21 (November 1936), 51-
        52 (M. S. Thesis Abstract).

681.   McLean, A. T.   "Shakespeare and Robert Greene:
        A Study of Seven Plays," Unpublished M. S. Thesis.
        University of Texas, 1937.

682.   McMillan, Mary Evelyn.   "An Edition of Greene's
        Vision and A Maiden's Dreame by Robert Greene,"
        Unpublished Ph. D. dissertation, University of Ala-
        bama, 1960.   [D. A. , 22 (1961), 1628-1629.]

103

683.   Mertins, O. "Robert Greene and the Plays of George-a-Greene," Breslau, 1885.

684.   Murphy, John Leo. "Some Problems in the Anonymous Drama of the Elizabethan Stage," Unpublished Ph. D. Dissertation, University of Oklahoma, 1963. [D. A. , 24 (1963), 3754.]

685.   Pearson, Lu. E. H. "The Love Conventions of the English Sonnet," Unpublished Ph. D. Dissertation, Stanford University, 1929. Abstracts of Dissertations (Stanford), (1929-1930), 50-57.

686.   Pennel, Charles Alexander. "Critical Edition of George-a-Greene, The Pinner of Wakefield," Unpublished Ph. D. Dissertation, University of Illinois, 1962. [D. A. , 23 (1962), 3890.]

687.   Potter, R. R. "Some Aspects of the Supernatural in English Comedy From the Origins to 1642," University of North Carolina Record, July 1926. pp. 42-45. (Abstract of Dissertation.)

688.   Saunders, Chauncy E. "Greene's Last Years," University of Chicago Abstracts of Theses. (Humanities Series), 5, 1929. pp. 487-491.

689.   Vincent, Charles J. "Natural History in the Works of Robert Greene," Harvard University Summaries of Theses, pp. 334-335.

F.　　Literary Background

690.　Aken, Andreas Rudolphus A. Van (ed.).　The En-
　　　cyclopedia of Classical Mythology.　Englewood
　　　Cliffs, N. J. :　Prentice-Hall, 1965.

691.　Applegate, James.　"The Classical Learning of Rob-
　　　ert Greene, " Bibliotheque de Humanisme et
　　　Renaissance, 28 (1966), 354-368.

692.　Baker, G. P.　"The Plays of the University Wits, "
　　　in CHEL V, Chapter VI, pp. 132-138.

693.　Baldwin, Charles Sears.　Renaissance Literary
　　　Theory and Practice.　Gloucester, Mass. :　Peter
　　　Smith, 1959 [c. 1939].　Chapters, I, II, V-VIII.

694.　Born, Adrianus Van den.　Encyclopedic Dictionary
　　　of the Bible, tr. Louis F. Hartman.　New York:
　　　McGraw-Hill, 1963.

695.　Bradner, Leicester.　"From Petrarch to Shakespeare, "
　　　in The Renaissance:　Six Essays ed.　The Metro-
　　　politan Museum of Art.　New York:　Harper and
　　　Row, 1962.　pp. 97-119.

696.　Burrage, Henry S. (ed.).　Early English and French
　　　Voyages Chiefly from Hakluyt 1534-1608.　New
　　　York:　Scribner's, 1906.

697.　Buttrick, George A.　et al (eds.).　The Interpreter's
　　　Dictionary of the Bible.　4 volumes.　New York:
　　　Abingdon Press, 1962.

698.　Chambers, E. K.　The Elizabethan Stage.　4 volumes.
　　　Oxford:　Clarendon Press, 1923.

699.　Day, Martin S.　"Sixteenth Century English Lan-
　　　guage, " in his History of English Literature to
　　　1660.　Garden City, New York:　Doubleday, 1963.
　　　pp. 137-143.

700.　De Santillana, Giorgio.　The Age of Adventure:　The
　　　Renaissance Philosophers.　New York:　New Ameri-
　　　can Library, 1959.

701.   Downer, Alan S.   The British Drama: A Handbook
        and Brief Chronicle. New York: Appleton-Cen-
        tury-Crofts, 1963.

702.   Fleay, Frederick Gard. A Chronicle History of the
        London Stage, 1559-1642. London: Reeves &
        Turner, 1890.

703.   Greenslade, S. L. (ed.). Cambridge History of the
        Bible: The West from the Reformation to the
        Present Day. Cambridge: University Press, 1963.

704.   Hall, Vernon, Jr.   Renaissance Literary Criticism:
        A Study of Its Social Content. Gloucester, Mass. :
        Peter Smith, 1959 [c. 1945].   pp. 229-231.

705.   Hardison, O. B. , Jr.   English Literary Criticism:
        The Renaissance. New York: Appleton-Century-
        Crofts, 1963.

706.   Hayashi, Tetsumaro.   "Thomas Lodge's Defence of
        Poetry," Concept, VI (Fall, 1968-69), 22-23.

707.   Herford, Charles Harold.   Studies In Literary Rela-
        tions of England and German in the Sixteenth
        Century. Cambridge: University Press, 1886.

708.   The Holy Bible (King James Version).   Cleveland:
        World Publishing Company, 1954.

709.   Harper's Topical Concordance, comp. by Charles R.
        Joy. New York: Harper, 1962.

710.   Jusserand, J. J.   The English Novel in the Time of
        Shakespeare.   tr. from the French by Elizabeth
        Lee.   4th ed.   London: T. F. Unwin, 1901.

711.   Knappen, M. M.   Tudor Puritanism: A Chapter in the
        History of Idealism.   Chicago: University of
        Chicago Press, 1965.

712.   Kraemer, Casper J. , Jr. (ed.).   The Complete Works
        of Horace. New York: Modern Library, 1936.

713.   Law, Robert Adger.   "A Looking Glasse and the
        Scriptures. " University of Texas Studies (1931),
        pp. 31-47.

714.   Lucie-Smith, Edward (ed.). The Penguin Book of
       Elizabethan Verse. Baltimore: Penguin Books,
       1956. pp. 11-21.

715.   Mackenzie, W. Roy. The English Moralities from
       the Point of Allegory. New York: Gordian Press,
       1966 [c. 1914].

716.   McNeal, Thomas H. "The Literary Origins of
       Robert Greene," Shakespeare Association Bulletin,
       14 (1939), 176-181.

717.   Murray, James A. H. et al (eds.). The Oxford
       English Dictionary. 13 volumes. Oxford: Claren-
       don Press, 1933.

718.   Nelson's Complete Concordance of the Revised Stand-
       ard Version Bible, compiled by John W. Ellison,
       New York: Thomas Nelson, 1957.

719.   Nicoll, Allardyce. British Drama. London: Harrap,
       1932.

720.   Parrott, Thomas Marc, and Ball, Robert Hamilton.
       A Short View of Elizabethan Drama. New York:
       Scribner's, 1958.

721.   Reed, Robert R. , Jr. The Occult in the Tudor and
       Stuart Stage. Boston: Christopher Publishing
       House, 1965. Passim.

722.   Ringler, William. "The First Phase of the Elizabethan
       Attack on the Stage, 1558-1579." Huntington Li-
       brary Quarterly, 5 (July 1942), 391-418.

723.   ----. "The Source of Lodge's Reply to Gosson's
       School of Abuse," RES, 25 (April 1939), 164-171.

724.   Rowse, A. L. The Expansion of Elizabethan England.
       New York: Harper and Row, 1955.

725.   Ryan, Pat M. , Jr. Thomas Lodge, Gentleman. Ham-
       den, Conn. : Shoe String Press, 1958.

726.   Schelling, Felix E. Foreign Influence in Elizabethan
       Plays. New York and London: (n. p.), 1923.

727.   Smith, Sir William. A Dictionary of Greek and
        Roman Antiquities. London: for Taylor & Walton,
        1842.

728.   ---- and Heseltine, Janet E. The Oxford Dictionary
        of English Proverbs. Oxford: Clarendon Press,
        1935.

729.   Spingarn, J. E. "Literary Criticism in England," in
        A History of Literary Criticism in the Renais-
        sance. New York: Harcourt, Brace, & World,
        1963. [c. 1899]. pp. 161-210.

730.   Taylor, Henry Osborn. "The Dramatic Self-Expres-
        sion of the Elizabethan Age," in his The English
        Mind, Volume IV of Thought and Expression in
        the Sixteenth Century. New York: Collier Books,
        1962 [c. 1930]. pp. 289-413.

731.   Thompson, Elbert N. S. The Controversy Between the
        Puritans and the Stage. New York: Henry Holt,
        1903.

732.   Tilley, Morris P. A Dictionary of Proverbs in Eng-
        land in the Sixteenth and Seventeenth Centuries.
        Ann Arbor: University of Michigan Press, 1950.

733.   Walker, William Sidney. A Critical Examination of
        the Text of Shakespeare, with Remarks on His
        Language and That of His Contemporaries, etc.
        3 volumes. London: John Russell Smith, 1860.

734.   White, Harold Ogden. Plagiarism and Imitation in
        the English Renaissance. Cambridge: University
        Press, 1935.

735.   Williamson, James A. The Age of Drake. 4th ed.
        New York: Barnes and Noble, 1960.

736.   Wimsatt, William K. , Jr. and Brooks, Cleanth. Lit-
        erary Criticism: A Short History. New York:
        Knopf, 1964.

737.   Wolff, Samuel Lee. "Robert Greene and the Italian
        Renaissance," English Studies, 37 (1907), 321-
        374.

738. Woodcock, P. G. *Short Dictionary of Mythology.*
     New York: Philosophical Library, 1953.

739. Wright, H. G. "Reply to W. L. Renwick's Greene's
     Ridstall Man," *MLR*, 30 (July 1935), 347.

740. Wright, Louis B. *Middle Class Culture in Eliza-
     bethan England.* University of North Carolina
     Press, 1935 [Reprinted by Cornell University
     Press, 1958]. *Passim.*

G.   Textual Problems

741.   Albright, Evelyn May. Dramatic Publication in
England, 1580-1640. New York: M. L. A. , 1927.

742.   Ames, Joseph. Typographical Antiquities; or an
Historical Account of the Origin and Progress of
Printing in Great Britain and Ireland. London:
Privately printed, 1785-90.

743.   Arber, Edward. The Term Catalogues, 1668-1709
A. D. 3 volumes. London: Privately printed,
1903-6.

744.   ---- (ed.). A Transcript of the Registers of the
Company of Stationers of London, 1554-1640 A. D.
5 volumes. London: Privately printed, 1875-
1894.

745.   Beloe, William. "Bibliographical Notes on Greene's
Works, " Anecdotes of Literature and Scarce
Books. London: Rivington, 1807-12, II, 168-
196.

746.   Bennett, Paul A. (ed.). Books and Printing: A
Treasury for Typophiles. Cleveland: World Pub-
lishing Company, 1951.

747.   Berereton, J. L. G. "Notes on Robert Greene and the
Editor from Birmingham," Beiblatt, 18 (February
1907), 46-62.

748.   Bishop, William W. (comp.). A Checklist of American Copies of Short-Title Catalogue Books. Ann
Arbor: University of Michigan Press, 1950.

749.   Blades, William. The Biography and Typography of
William Caxton. New York: Scribner and Wel-
ford, 1882.

750.   Bowers, Fredson, Principles of Bibliographical Des-
cription. Princeton University Press, 1949.

751.   Bradley, Henry. "Some Textual Puzzles in Greene's
       Works," MLR, 1 (April 1905), 208-211.

752.   The British Museum. Facsimiles from Early Printed
       Books in the British Museum. London: British
       Museum, 1897.

753.   ----. A Guide to the Exhibition in the King's Li-
       brary, Illustrating the History of Printing, Music-
       printing, and Bookbinding. London: British
       Museum, 1926.

754.   Brooke, C. F. Tucker. "The Authorship of 2 & 3
       Henry VI," The Tudor Drama. A History of Eng-
       lish National Drama to the Retirement of Shake-
       speare. Boston: Houghton, Mifflin, 1911.

755.   Collier, John Payne, (ed.). Extracts from the Reg-
       isters of the Stationers' Company of Works Engered
       for Publication Between the Years 1557 and 1570,
       with notes and illustrations. Volumes I and II.
       London: Shakespeare Society, 1848 and 1849.
       (* Nos. 38 and 41.)

756.   Dawson, Giles E. , and Laetitia, Kennedy-Skipton.
       Elizabethan Handwriting 1500-1650, a Manual.
       New York: Norton, 1966.

757.   Deighton, Kenneth. The Old Dramatists Conjectural
       Readings of Marston, etc. Westminster: Archi-
       bald Constable, 1896. pp. 180-187.

758.   Duff, Edward Gordon. Early English Printing, a
       Series of Facsimiles of All the Types Used in
       England during the 15th Century, etc. with an
       Introduction. London: K. Paul, Trench, Trubner,
       1896.

759.   ----. Early Printed Books (A Volume of Books about
       Books, ed. A. W. Pollard.) London: K. Paul,
       Trench, Trubner & Co. , 1893.

760.   ----. Fifteenth Century English Books. London:
       Bibliographical Society, 1917.

761.   ----. The Printers, Stationers, and Bookbinders of
       Westminster and London from 1476-1535. Cam-

bridge: University Press, 1906.

762.   English Books 1475-1640: Consolidated Cross Index
       by STC Numbers, Years 1-19. Ann Arbor, Mich-
       igan: University of Microfilms, 1956.

763.   Greg, Walter W. A Bibliography of the English
       Printed Drama to the Restoration. Volume I:
       Stationers' Records: Plays to 1616, Nos. 1-349.
       London: Bibliographical Society, 1939.

764.   ----. A Bibliography of the English Printed Drama
       to the Restoration. London: Printed for the Bib-
       liographical Society at the University Press, 1939.
       Vol. I, Passim.

765.   ----. The Editorial Problem in Shakespeare. Oxford:
       Clarendon Press, 1954.

766.   ----. "J. C. Collins's The Plays and Poems of
       Robert Greene." MLR, I (April 1906), 238-251.

767.   Halliday, F. E. A Shakespeare Companion, 1550-
       1950. London: Gerald Duckworth, 1952.

768.   Harbottle, Thomas B. Dictionary of Quotations:
       Classical. London: Sonnenschein, 1897.

769.   Harington, John. An Apologie for Poetrie. London:
       n. p. , 1590.

770.   Hastings, James. Dictionary of the Bible. 5 volumes.
       New York: Scribner's, 1898-1904.

771.   Hatch, O. L. "The Source and Authorship of The
       Thracian Wonder," MLN, 23 (January 1908), 16-
       20.

772.   Johnson, John. Typographia or the Printer's Instruc-
       tor. 2 volumes. London: (Privately printed),
       1824.

773.   Jones. Hugh P. A New Dictionary of Foreign Phrases
       and Classical Quotations. Edinburgh: C. W. Dea-
       con, 1918.

774.   Law, Robert A.   "J. C. Collins's edition of The
        Plays and Poems of Robert Greene," MLN, 22
        (June 1907), 197-199.

775.   Lee, Jane.   "The Authorship of the Second and Third
        Parts of Henry VI and the Originals," in The
        New Shakespeare Transactions, 1875-76.   p. 219.

776.   McKerrow, Ronald B. (ed.).   A Dictionary of Print-
        ers and Booksellers in England, Scotland, and
        Ireland, and of Foreign Printers of English Books,
        1557-1640.   London: Bibliographical Society, 1910.

777.   ----.   "Edward Allde as a Typical Trade Printer,"
        Library, 10 (1929-30), 121-162.

778.   ----.   "The Elizabethan Printers and Dramatic Manu-
        scripts," Library, (London), 12 (December 1931),
        253-275.

779.   ----.   An Introduction to Bibliography for Literary
        Students.   Oxford: Clarendon Press, 1927.

780.   ----.   Printers' and Publishers' Devices in England
        and Scotland 1485-1640.   London: Bibliographical
        Society, 1949.

781.   ----, and Ferguson, F. S. Title-page Borders Used
        in England and Scotland, 1485-1640.   London:
        Oxford University Press for the Bibliographical
        Society, 1932.
        (* Ferguson, F. S.   Additions to Title-Page Bor-
        ders, 1485-1640.   London: Bibliographical Society,
        1936.)

782.   Mantinband, James H. (ed.).   Dictionary of Latin
        Literature.   New York: Philosophical Library,
        1956.

783.   Maxwell, J. C.   "An Emendation in Greene," N & Q,
        205 (January 1960), 37.

784.   Morrison, Paul G.   Index of Printers, Publishers and
        Booksellers.   Charlottesville: Bibliographical
        Society of the University of Virginia, 1950.

785. Moxon, Joseph. Mechanick Exercises: or, the Doc-
      trine of Handy-works. Applied to the Art of
      Printing. Volume II. London: J. Maxon, 1683.

786. Murray, Sir James A. H. , et al (eds.). A New
      English Dictionary on Historical Principles. Ox-
      ford: Clarendon Press, 1933.

787. Oliphant, E. H. "Elizabethan Problems of Author-
      ship," MP, 8 (January 1911), 411-459.

788. Parr, Johnstone, and Shapiro, I. A. Instructions to
      Editors of the Works of Robert Greene. Birming-
      ham, England: Shakespeare Society, University
      of Birmingham, 1959.

789. ----, et al. List of Editions, Copies and Locations
      of the Works of Robert Greene. Shakespeare
      Institute, 1958.

790. Pollard, Alfred W. (ed.). Bibliographica. Papers
      on Books Their History and Art. 3 volumes.
      London: 1895-1897.

791. ----. Shakespeare Folios and Quarto, A Study in the
      Bibliography of Shakespeare's Plays, 1594-1685.
      London: Methuen, 1909.

792. ----, and Redgrave, G. R. A Short-Title Catalogue
      of Books Printed in England, Scotland, and Ireland
      and of English Books Printed Abroad, 1475-1640.
      London: Bibliographical Society, 1946.

793. Reed, Talbot Baines. A History of the Old English
      Letter Foundries. London: Elliot Stock, 1887.

794. Sanders, Norman. "Robert Greene's Way with a
      Source," N & Q, 14 (March 1967), 89-91.

795. Saunders, Chauncey Elwood. "Robert Greene and
      His Editions," PMLA, 48 (June 1933), 392-417.

796. Sawyer, C. J. and Darton, F. J. H. "Robert Greene
      and the Book-Collector," English Books, 1475-
      1900. Westminster: [n. p.], 1927. I, 67-72.

797.   Schoeck, R. J. (ed.). Editing Sixteenth Century
       Texts. University of Toronto Press for the Edit-
       orial Conference Committee of the University of
       Toronto, 1966. pp. 13, 15, 18.

798.   Smith, G. C. M.   "Two Emendations," N & Q, 117
       (April 18, 1908), 302.

799.   Southward, John. Modern Printings, a Handbook of
       the Principles and Practice of Typography and the
       Auxiliary Arts. London: Raithby, Lawrence,
       1912-13.

800.   Tannenbaum, S. A.   "The Handwriting of Robert
       Greene," The Booke of Sir Thomas More. New
       York: Tenny Press, 1927. p. 78.

801.   Timperley, C. H.   A Dictionary of Printers and Print-
       ing. London: H. Johnson, 1939.

802.   University Microfilms, Inc.   See English Books 1475-
       1640.

803.   Updike, Daniel Berkeley.   Printing Types, Their
       History, Forms, and Use, a Study in Survivals.
       2 volumes. Cambridge: Harvard University Press,
       1922.

804.   Webster's Biographical Dictionary. Springfield, Mass. :
       Merriam, 1943.

805.   Webster's Georgraphical Dictionary. Springfield,
       Mass. : Merriam, 1949.

806.   Zimmerman, J. E.   Dictionary of Classical Mythology.
       New York: Harper and Row, 1964.

H. Bibliography (A List of Reference Books Consulted)

Abstracts of English Studies.

Annual Bibliography of English Language and Literature.

Baker, G. P. , "Plays of the University Wits ...
    Bibliography," CHEL, V, Chapter VI, 418-419.

Books in Print

The British Museum General Catalogue of Printed
    Books.

The Cambridge Bibliography of English Literature.

Cole, G. B. "Bibliography . . . a Forecast," Trans-
    actions of the Bibliographical Society of America,
    14 (1920).

Cumulative Book Index.

The Dictionary of National Biography (DNB).

Education Index.

Essays and General Literature Index.

International Index to Periodicals (now Humanities and
    Social Science Index).

Johnson, Robert C. The University Wits: Lyly,
    Greene, Peele, Nashe and Lodge (London: Nether
    Press, 1969).

Jordan, John Clark. "Bibliography," in his Robert
    Greene. New York: Octagon Books, 1965.
    [c. 1915]. pp. 221-225.

Library of Congress Catalog of Printed Cards.

The National Union Catalog.

Nineteenth Century Reader's Guide to Periodical Literature.

Parr, Johnstone, and Shapiro, I. A. Instructions to Editors of the Works of Robert Greene. Birmingham, England: Shakespeare Institute, University of Birmingham, 1959.

Parr, Johnstone, et al (eds.). List of Editions, Copies and Locations of the Works of Robert Greene. Shakespeare Institute, 1958.

PMLA (Annual Bibliography).

The Reader's Adviser, ed. by Hester R. Hoffman.

Reader's Guide to Periodical Literature.

Ribner, Irving. Tudor and Stuart Drama. New York: Appleton-Century-Crofts, 1966.

Smith, Gordon Ross. A Classified Shakespeare Bibliography, 1936-1956. University Park: Pennsylvania State University Press, 1963.

SP (Annual Bibliography).

Subject Guide to Books in Print.

Tannenbaum, Samuel A. Robert Greene: A Concise Bibliography. New York: S. A. Tannenbaum. 1945.

----, and Dorothy R. Supplement to a Bibliography of Robert Greene. New York: S. A. Tannenbaum, 1945.

PART III: APPENDICES

A. Key to Abbreviations

CHEL= Cambridge History of English Literature.

DA= Dissertation Abstracts.

DD= Doctoral Dissertations Accepted by American University-
   sities.

DNB= Dictionary of National Biography.

EA= Études Anglaises.

ELH= Journal of English Literary History.

ELN= English Language Notes.

ES= English Studies

HLQ= Huntington Library Quarterly.

Index= Index to Theses Accepted for Higher Degrees in the
   Universities of Great Britain and Ireland.

JEGP= Journal of English and German Philology.

MLN= Modern Language Notes.

MLQ= Modern Language Quarterly.

MLR= Modern Language Review.

MP= Modern Philology.

n. d. = no date.

N & Q= Notes and Queries.

n. p. = no publisher mentioned or identified.

PBSA= Papers of the Bibliographical Society of America.

PMLA= Publications of the Modern Language Association of
America.

PQ= Philological Quarterly.

RES= Review of English Studies

SB= Studies in Bibliography.

SNL= Shakespeare Newsletter.

SP= Studies in Philology.

SR= Stationers' Register (entered in S. R.).

STC= Short-Title Catalogue of English Books Printed in
England, Scotland, and Ireland and of English Books
Printed Abroad, 1475-1640. London: Bibliographical
Society, 1926.

TLS= Times (London) Literary Supplement.

YWES= The Year's Work in English Studies.

B.   A List of Periodicals and Newspapers Indexed

Academy.

Anglia (Zeitschrift fur Englische Philologie)
(Germany)

Athenaeum (England).

Baconiana (England).

Biographia Dramatica (London, England).

Bibliotheque d'Humanisme et Renaissance (France).

Book Lore (London, England).

Bookman (London, England).

Boston University Studies in English.

Comparative Literature.

Concept. (Missouri).

Convivium (Italy).

Dial.

Dramatic Monthly.

Dublin Review (Ireland).

Durham University Journal.

Edinburgh Review (Scotland).

Emporia State Research Studies.

English Language Notes.

English Language Notes.

English Studies (Netherland).

Etudes Anglaises (France).

Explicator.

Hobbies.

Huntington Library Quarterly.

Indian Journal of English Studies (India).

Irish Monthly Magazine (Ireland).

Journal of English and Germanic Philology.

Journal of English Literary History.

Library (England)

Lumina (Japan).

Manchester Quarterly (England).

Modern Language Notes.

Modern Language Quarterly.

Modern Language Review.

Modern Philology.

Nation.

New Monthly Magazine (London, England).

New Statesman.

New Zealand Magazine (New Zealand).

Notes and Queries (England).

Papers of the Bibliographical Society of America.

Philologia Pragensia (Now Casopis Pro Moderrni Filologii) (Czechoslovakia).

Philological Quarterly.

PMLA.

Reading College Review.

Review of English Studies (England).

Review of Literary Criticism.

Revue des Langues Vivantes (Brussels, Belgium).

Shakespeare Association Bulletin.

Shakespeare Jahrbuch (Germany).

Shakespeare Newsletter.

Shakespeare Quarterly.

Shakespeare Survey (England).

Spectator (England).

Studies in Bibliography.

Studies in English Literature, 1500-1900.

Studies in Philology.

Times (London) Literary Supplement (England).

University of Texas Studies in English.

Victorian Poetry.

Year's Work in English Studies.

AUTHOR INDEX

Name	Sequence Number
Bentley, Gerald Eades	119, 623
Berereton, John Le Gay	284, 477, 478, 665, 747
Berkenhourt, John	624
Bishop, William Warner.	748
Black, Matthew.	367
Blades, William	749
Bluestone, Max (ed.)	76, 368, 517
Boas, Frederick S.	479, 480, 625
Bond, R. Warwick	120
Born, Adrianus Van den.	694
Bottrall, M. (comp.)	481
Bovinski, Ludwig	121, 437, 482
Bowers, Fredson	483, 750
Bradbrook, Muriel C..	69, 98, 122, 220, 291, 484, 485, 486, 487
Bradley, Henry.	488, 751
Bradley, J. F.	489
Bradner, Leicester	695
Brandes, G. (ed)	308
Bratchell, D. F. (ed.)	5, 324, 329
Briscoe, J. P. (ed.)	398
British Museum.	752, 753

Name	Sequence Number
Brooke, C. F. Tucker	70, 123, 124, 237, 253, 292, 490, 491, 626, 754
Brown, G. A.	55
Brown, J. M.	125, 221
Brown, John Russell (ed.)	126, 189, 399
Browne, C. E.	492
Brydges Sir Samuel E.	400
Budd, Laurence	254, 330, 493
Buland, M.	396
Bullen, A. H. (ed.)	38, 627
Burrage, Henry S. (ed.)	696
Busby, Olive Mary	370
Bush, Douglas	401, 494
Butler, P.	127
Buttrick, G. A. (ed.)	697
Camden, C.	128
Camp, C. W.	495
Campbell, Oscar J. (ed.)	636
Carpenter, F. I.	402
Carroll, William M.	438, 497
Cartwright, Robert	496
Castle, E. J.	498
Cawley, Robert R.	499, 628

Name	Sequence Number
Cowl, R. P.	132
Cowling, G. H.	407
Craig, Hardin	133, 508
Crane, T. F.	509
Crawford, Chas.	352, 353
Creizenach, W.	510
Cruttwell, Patrick	408
Cunliffe, J. W.	354, 373, 374
Curry, John V.	511
Curtis, G. B.	362
Darton, F. J. H.	760
Daughhetee, Catherine	p. xii
Dawson, Giles E.	756
Day, Martin S.	57, 75, 224, 512, 631, 699
Dean, James S., Jr.	326, 327, 513
Deighton, Kenneth	757
Delius, M.	309
Dent, Robert W.	50, 134, 280
De Perott, J.	135
De Santillana, Giorgia	700
Dewar, R.	632
Dickinson, Thomas H. (ed.).	9, 10, 514

Name	Sequence Number
Disraeli, Issac	409
Dodsley, R. (ed.)	11
Doherty, Paul Colman	677
Dorsch, T. S. (tr.)	372
Downer, Alan S.	515, 701
Drake, N.	136
Drew, Philip	137, 225, 633
Drinkwater, J.	410
Duff, Edward Gordon	758, 759, 760, 761
Dunham, S. A.	601, 634
Dunlop, J.	439
Dyce, Alexander	12, 13, 516
Eagle, Solomon (ed.)	233
Ekelbald, Inga-Stine	138, 355
Ellis-Fermor, Una M.	76, 139, 240, 375
Ellison, John W. (comp.)	718
Empson, William	77, 376, 411, 517
Erskine, John	412, 635
Esler, Anthony	518
Evans, Sir Ifor	519
Fansler, Harriott Ely	520
Farmer, John S. (ed.)	14

Name	Sequence Number
Farnharm, Willard	521
Ferguson, F. S.	781
Fleay, Frederick G.	78, 140, 377, 522, 523, 702
Fluchere, Henri	524
Ford, Boris (ed.)	259, 525
Forsythe, R. S.	141
Freebury, Victor Oscar.	526
Freeman, Arthur	527, 528
Frost, David L.	194
Gaw, Allison	142
Gayley, Charles Mills	45, 79, 101, 241, 260, 295, 356, 529, 637
Gerrard, E. A.	378
Gibson, J. P. S. R.	530
Goree, Roselle Gould	440
Gosse, Edmund W. (ed.)	15, 143, 531, 638
Graves, Thornton S.	144
Gray, H. D.	145
Greene, H. W.	261
Greenslade, S. L. (ed.).	703

Name	Sequence Number
Hudson, Ruth	243
Hurrell, J. D.	446
Hunter, G. K.	462
Ing, Catherine	416, 543
Ingleby, C. M. (comp.)	195, 500
Jackson, W. A. (ed.)	333
Jenkins, Harold	226, 347
Jewkes, Wilfred T.	544
Johnson, Francis R.	59
Johnson, John	772
Johnson, Robert C.	p. ix
Johnson, W. N.	382
Jones, F. L.	52
Jones, Hugh P.	773
Jordan, John Clark	46, 53, 60, 65, 81, 103, 157, 227, 244, 266, 278, 282, 286, 298, 310, 328, 335, 348, 359, 669
Joseph, Sister Miriam	545
Joy, Charles R. (comp.)	713
Judges, A. V. (ed.)	27, 447, 546
Jusserand, J. J.	28, 448, 710

Name	Sequence Number
Keltie, J. S. (ed.)	29
Kendall, Jack L.	679
Kennedy, H. A.	159
Kettner, Eugene J.	160
Klein, David	383, 547
Knapp, M.	287
Knappen, M. M.	711
Kocher, P. H.	680
Koeppel, E.	360
Kozmian, Stanislaus	311
Kraemer, Casper J., Jr. (ed.)	712
Krapp, G. P.	449
Kunitz, Stanley J. (ed.)	647
Landt, D. B.	161
Langbaine, G.	417
Lavin, J. A.	418, 450, 548
Law, Robert A.	162, 267, 268, 713, 774
Lawlor, John	312, 451
Lee, Elizabeth (tr.)	28, 30, 710
Lee, Jane	775
Lee, Sidney	419, 549
Lemmi, C. W.	299

Name	Sequence Number
Lewis, C. S.	550, 648
Lievsay, John Leon.	163, 551, 552, 649
Locke, I. G.	397
Lodge, Thomas	31
Lucie-Smith, Edward (ed.)	40, 714
McCallum, J. D.	82
McGinn, Donald J.	164, 336
MacIlwraith, Archibald K. (ed.). . . .	32
Mackenzie, W. Roy.	715
McKerrow, Ronald B.	553, 776, 777, 778, 779, 780, 781
MacLaine, A. H.	83, 245
McLean, A. T.	681
McMillan, Mary Evelyn.	33, 279, 365, 682
McNeal, Thomas H.	165, 228, 229, 313, 554, 716
McNeir, Waldo F.	84, 166, 167, 168, 169, 246, 269, 300, 325, 366, 555
Manly, John Matthews	247, 556
Mantinband, James H. (ed.).	782
Marder, Louis	p. xi, p. xii, 170, 230, 452

Name	Sequence Number
Maxwell, B.	558
Maxwell, J. C.	559, 783
Mertins, O.	683
The Metropolitan Museum of Art (ed.)	695
Meynell, (Mrs.) A. C. T.	420
Mildenberger, K.	650
Miller, Edwin H.	61, 62, 171, 172, 173, 337, 338, 339, 340, 349, 560
Miller, E. Madge	561, 651
Mills, J. W.	85
Mills, L. J.	562
Minto, W.	421
Mithal, H. S. D.	563
Moon, Eric.	p. xii
Moore, J. R.	422
Moorman, F. W.	314
Morley, H. (ed.)	315, 564
Morris, Helen	565
Morrison, Morris R.	301
Morrison, Paul G.	784
Mosley, Edwin M. (ed.)	432

Name	Sequence Number
Moulton, C. W.	566
Moxon, Joseph	785
Muir, Kenneth	47, 86, 174, 248, 270, 302, 384, 567
Mukherjee, Sujit Kumar	303
Murphy, D.	175
Murphy, John Leo	684
Murray, Sir James A. H. (ed.). . . .	717, 786
Mustard, W. P.	385
Nathanson, Leonard.	341
Needleman, M. H.	570
Neilson, William Allan (ed.)	568
Nelson, Malcolm A.	104
Nicholson, B.	105
Nicholson, W.	316
Nicoll, Allardyce.	719
Norman, Charles.	176
O'Conner, J. J.	569
Oldys, W. (ed.)	342
Oliphant, E. H. C. (ed.)	177, 787
Oliver, Leslie M.	363
Oras, Ants	386

Name	Sequence Number
Otis, William Bradley	570
Pafford, J. H. P. (ed.)	178, 317
Paradise, N. Burton	179, 271, 571, 652
Park, T. (ed.)	342
Parker, R. B.	343, 344
Parr, Johnstone	p. vii, p. ix, p. xi, p. xii, 180, 331, 653, 670, 671, 788, 789
Parrott, Thomas M.	87, 387, 572, 654, 720
Pearson, Lu Emily H.	423, 685
Pearson, Terry P.	63
Peers, E. A.	304
Pennel, Charles A.	106, 181, 686
Pickering, W.	34
Pierce, F. E.	318
Pollard, Alfred W. (ed.)	790, 791, 792
Porter, C.	319
Potter, R. R.	687
Price, Ward T.	655
Quaintance, Richard E., Jr.	288, 576
Quiller-Couch, A.	320
Quinn, Edward G. (ed.)	636

Name	Sequence Number
Rabkin, Norman (ed.)	76, 517
Rae, Wesley D.	272, 577, 656
Reardsibm, J. P. (ed.)	424
Reed, Robert R., Jr.	88, 578, 721
Reed, Talbot Baines	425, 793
Renner, Dick A.	p. xi
Renwick, W. L.	579
Rhys, E.	426
Ribner, Irving	p. ix, 117, 182, 361, 580, 581
Ringler, William	722, 723
Ristine, F. H.	388
Robertson, John M.	183, 184, 185, 186, 187, 584
Rollins, Hyder E. (ed.)	41
Rossiter, A. P.	585
Roston, Murray	273, 389
Round, Percy Z.	89
Routh, Harold V.	453, 586
Rowland, Samuel (ed.)	35
Rowse, A. L.	188, 724
Ryan, Pat M., Jr.	725
Salingar, L. G.	462

Name	Sequence Number
Smith, G. C. M.	199, 798
Smith, G. Gregory (ed.)	153, 289, 599
Smith, Sir William	727, 728
Soellner, Rolf	306
South, Helen P.	200, 232
Southward, John	799
Spencer, Hazelton (ed.)	600
Spencer, Theodore	601
Spens, J.	201
Spingarn, J. E.	729
Squire, Sir John Collings	233
Staton, Walter F., Jr.	456
Staunton, H.	202
Storojenko, Nicholas	142, 290, 660, 673
Sutherland, James	457
Swaen, A. E. H.	275
Swinburne, A. C.	204
Sykes, H. Dugdale	108, 205
Symonds, John A.	206, 391
Talbert, Ernest W.	207, 392
Tannenbaum, Samuel A.	p. viii, p xi, 249, 800

Name	Sequence Number
Winstanley, W.	463
Wolff, Samuel Lee	464, 737
Wood, Anthony	664
Woodberry, G. E.	393, 394
Woodcock, P. G.	738
Woodward, Parker	615
Wright, Celeste Turner	215
Wright, H. G.	616, 739
Wright, Louis B.	617, 618, 740
Wynne, Arnold	216, 395
Zimmerman, J. E.	806